A Study in Friendship

Saint Robert Southwell and Henry Garnet

D1564644

*Nineteen hundred and ninety-five
marks the four hundredth anniversary
of the martyrdom of Saint Robert Southwell
at Tyburn.*

*In sixteen hundred and six
Henry Garnet was executed
at St. Paul's Churchyard.*

Philip Caraman, S.J.

A Study in Friendship

Saint Robert Southwell and Henry Garnet

THE INSTITUTE OF JESUIT SOURCES
1995

Number 16 in Series IV: Studies on Jesuit Topics

© The Institute of Jesuit Sources
3700 West Pine Boulevard
Saint Louis MO 63108
Tel: [314] 977-7257
Fax: [314] 977-7263

Library of Congress Catalogue Card Number 95-80587
ISBN 1-880810-15-8

CONTENTS

Preface

This small book took its present shape in slow stages, but at no time was it envisaged as a formal biography of Robert Southwell. Eventually it became a kind of character study or an attempt to enter into the mind and heart of a brilliant, attractive, and astonishingly brave young Elizabethan Jesuit, who was also a poet, a master of prose, and a martyr.

Among the many things that drew me to Robert Southwell was his remarkable capacity for friendship, a matter on which he dwells in his verse, his prose works, his meditations, and his letters. In 1955, while doing research in the central Jesuit archives in Rome, I had the good fortune to come across a large number of hitherto unknown letters of his and still more of his friend and companion Henry Garnet. Thus I found myself in possession of a rich seam of historical material that documented one of the most moving friendships in the Elizabethan era. It was a friendship based on the shared experience of mortal danger and a common ideal of religious profession. The only comparison that has since suggested itself to me is the close understanding that bound St. Ignatius of Loyola, the founder of the Society of Jesus, to St. Francis Xavier, the apostle of the Indies and his favorite companion.

In sketching the unfolding of this friendship, I have touched on many other aspects of Southwell's character, not least his physical courage that won the unstinted admiration of his cousin, Sir Robert Cecil, and of Queen Elizabeth I herself, the playmate of his mother.

For the most part I have let Southwell himself reveal his aspirations, his moments of excitement, and his alternating moods of depression and exaltation—in fact, all that made him such a saintly, human, and endearing friend of all. A young man of great sensitivity, he found his heroism put in almost too sharp a focus by the sometimes cruel age in which he lived.

Southwell's father had established his position in the realm under Henry VIII, who is now acknowledged to have put to death a proportionately larger number of his subjects than did Stalin in our own time. His daughter Mary I, a merciful person by temperament, found herself enforcing laws of an earlier era under which close on three hundred of her subjects were burned at the stake, including a simple soul like Hugh Latimer, Nicholas Ridley, who as bishop of London under Edward VI did much to improve the condition of the poor, and Thomas Cranmer, whose fate it was to see half a dozen sides to every question. Though the men and women who suffered under Mary were fewer than those put to death under similar laws on the Continent, it was something unprecedented in England.

Mary's half sister, Elizabeth I, was determined not to make martyrs for religion. Only by means of an act of Parliament (27 Eliz. c. 2) making it treachery for native-born Englishmen to return as priests to their own country after receiving Holy Orders abroad was her government able to present them as disloyal subjects. It is essential to appreciate this in order to understand Southwell's plight on stepping ashore secretly at

Folkestone, his impassioned defense of his former students at the English College, Rome, and the manner of his brutal execution. He was suffering the death that the statute book of medieval England reserved for treachery.

If Henry Garnet plays the lesser role in this study, he nevertheless forms the perfect foil to Southwell's character: he was so attached to his companion that when he was left without him, he seems to have suffered a breakdown from which he took some months to recover. While Southwell's poems form a considerable part of this book, they are set in the framework of Garnet's letters. For the most part I have left each to speak for himself. The reader will see at once that there is nothing sentimental in their friendship: it was a deep-rooted human affection balanced by a shared burning zeal for the kingdom of God on earth that brought them together.

Garnet's letters with a few exceptions are translated from the Latin, for they are mostly reports written to his superior in Rome, Claudio Aquaviva, the Jesuit general. Southwell, on the other hand, speaks in the language of Shakespeare: he moved in his circle and may possibly have known him. Like Shakespeare's, his language is young, harmonious, freshly forged, and filled with fire.

Both principals in this book have a message for today. As the Iron Curtain between East and West Europe was raised, the same story unfolded: concentration camps, forced confessions, physical torture, psychological pressure—all endured by loyal citizens branded as enemies to the state. The story told here is sadly repeated also in the Far East.

ABBREVIATIONS USED
IN THE FOOTNOTES

Persons

C.A.: Claudio Aquaviva

H.G.: Henry Garnet

R.S.: Robert Southwell

W.W.: William Weston

Books

C.R.S.: Catholic Record Society

Devlin: Christopher Devlin, S.J. *The Life of Robert Southwell, Poet and Martyr.* Longmans, 1956

Epistle of Comfort: Robert Southwell. *An Epistle of Comfort.* Edited by Margaret Waugh; foreword by Philip Caraman, S.J. Burns and Oates, 1956

Humble Supplication: Robert Southwell. *An Humble Supplication to Her Majestie.* Edited by R. C. Bold. Cambridge University Press, 1953

McDonald: James H. McDonald. *The Poems and Prose Writings of Robert Southwell, S.J.: A Bibliographical Study.* Oxford University Press, 1937

Poems: *The Poems of Robert Southwell, S.J.* Edited by James H. McDonald and Nancy Pollard Brown. Oxford University Press, 1967

Spiritual Exercises and Devotions: Robert Southwell, S.J. *Spiritual Exercises and Devotions.* Edited by J. M. de Buck, S.J. Sheed and Ward, 1931

W.W.: *The Autobiography of an Elizabethan.* William Weston. Translated and edited by Philip Caraman, S.J. Longmans, 1955

Philip Caraman, S.J. *Henry Garnet 1555-1606 and the Gunpowder Plot.* Longmans, 1953

F.G.: Fondo Gesuito 651

The reference is to a volume of letters in the central Jesuit archives in Rome. As these letters are arranged alphabetically and according to date, I have thought it better not to give the numbers of the letters, which are confusing and unnecessary for reference.

ONE

IF YOU LOVE A FRIEND

On May 8, 1586, the feast of St. Michael, two young Englishmen, both Jesuits, Robert Southwell and Henry Garnet, might have been seen together on the Milvian Bridge, two miles up the Tiber from the center of Rome. It was about dawn. They were taking their leave of an older-looking priest, Robert Persons, who had ridden out with them. For two years Persons had been working for this day, overcoming resistance in high places to the enterprise on which the two younger men were now setting out. It was the last time he was to see them. Their destination was England. "Two arrows shot at the same mark," Southwell had said, concealing his fears under cover of a jest, as he was sometimes known to do. He meant that if one of them was caught and hanged, the other might get away.[1]

A month before this leave-taking, they had received instructions from the superior general of the Jesuits, Claudio Aquaviva, a Neapolitan: he had more discerningly spoken of them as lambs dispatched to the slaughter. It required no great prescience on his part to forecast their fate. In an age when an unsought and

---

[1] Footnote in an unknown hand attached to a letter of H.G. to C.A. (March 10, 1594), F.G. 651.

unprovoked martyr's death was highly prized, he might
have said this with a tinge of envy, for the Superior
General had once offered himself for this mission and
had been refused.

The briefing he gave them would salve their conscience but would do nothing to save their lives. They
were not to meddle in the affairs of state; in their reports to Rome, they were to avoid political news and
gossip; in company they were to shun all talk about the
Queen and were not to countenance it in others. Instead, they were to write about themselves and about
each other. Aquaviva knew them both well, especially
Henry Garnet, who had lived with him under the same
roof and had often assisted him at Mass whenever
there were crowds of worshippers to communicate.[2]

Before giving them his parting blessing, Persons
had a request to make: that on their arrival in England,
they would seek out his old mother, who lived in Som-
erset, and care for her if there was anything she might
need. He then blessed them and turned back to Rome.

The road Garnet chose was not the direct way
north along the Via Cassia but the old Via Caecilia
that cut directly across the Apennines to the Adriatic.
He and Southwell wanted first to pray to the Blessed
Virgin of Loreto. The shrine lay about two miles from
the town of Ancona high above the sea. For nearly
three centuries it had attracted the devotion of innu-
merable saints. In more recent times St. Francis Xavier
had prayed there twice, the first time with St. Ignatius
on his way to Rome to seek confirmation of his Society,
the second time before setting out for the Indies. On
that occasion he had offered Mass in the Holy House,
which according to popular belief angels had trans-
ported there from Nazareth. Then he had felt the

---

[2] C.R.S., 5:361f.

Blessed Virgin breathing into his soul such zeal that it made India and the whole world too small a compass for his apostolate.

It was the same inspiration that Southwell now sought from Loreto. Coming as he did from close to the shrine of our Lady at Walsingham, he had special cause to honor her. Later, or perhaps even now, he addressed her in a poem that was first published in 1595:

> For God on earth she is the royal throne,
> The chosen cloth to make his mortal weed;
> The quarry to cut our corner-stone
>
> . . . .
>
> The child of man, the parent of a God.[3]

The long journey ahead of the two priests gave them the opportunity to know each other's fears, aspirations, moods, and temper. Although they had been together in Rome some years, it was during these months on the road to Flanders that the two young men formed what must be the best-documented friendship in Elizabethan annals.

Friendship had been the subject of notes that Southwell made eight years earlier when he had been a novice at Sant'Andrea on the Quirinal. He had then written these words in his journal:

If you love a friend so much, if he or she is so attractive that everything he asked of you, you would agree to; and if it is so sweet to sit and talk with him, describe your mishaps to him—then with how much more trust should you betake yourself to God, the God of goodness, converse with him, show him your weakness and distress, for he has greater care of you than you have of yourself, indeed he is more intimately you than you are.[4]

---

[3] *Poems,* 4.

[4] *Spiritual Exercises and Devotions,* section 25, p. 66.

Unquestioning trust was needed between the two priests in the work that had been assigned them. Their backgrounds in the stratified society of the day were sharply contrasted. The Southwells, like their cousins, the Cecils and the Howards, had established their fortunes on the spoils of the monasteries. Robert's grandfather, a commissioner for the closure of religious houses, had acquired four monastic properties, including Horsham St. Faith, once a Benedictine priory, where Robert was born at the end of 1561, a year after Princess Elizabeth ascended the throne. Even then there were still some old monks to be found in the countryside living on state pensions rendered nugatory by inflation.

Robert had inherited uncommon good looks, already apparent in his cradle. The story was told that a gypsy woman, captivated by his appearance, kidnapped the infant from its nursery. He grew up to be a lonely, moody youth, out of sympathy with the worldly aspirations of his father. "Even from my earliest infancy," he once wrote to his father, "you were wont in merriment to call me Father Robert."[5] Ambition had spurred his grandfather, but it was alien to him: Robert compared it to "a crocodile that groweth (according to the legend) as long as it liveth." It was clear to all that he had no interest in money making. From childhood his thoughts were remote from mundane affairs. As he expressed it himself,

> I have no care of coin.
> Well-doing is my life.
> My mind to me an empire is
> While grace affordeth health.[6]

---

[5] J. W. Trotman, *The Triumphs over Death* (London, 1914), 43.

[6] *Poems,* 67.

As he now rode north, he recalled the sights of his youth. "See what happened in England, in Germany or anywhere else, where nowadays for most people the names of 'monk' and 'scoundrel' have the same meaning. And it is true that even daily we see numbers of them roaming from place to place, to the grave discredit of religion."[7] It was a sight that had determined him to make manifest in his own conduct the *Res Christiana* by gentleness of manners and the fire of charity.

This was the inspiration of his religious vocation when he was at the English school at Douai, where his father, still loyal at least in sympathy to the old faith, had sent him for his education. This same gentleness and fire remained with him to the end.

His companion, Garnet, had nothing quixotic in his make-up, but he possessed a like gentleness with almost unlimited patience. Exact, judicious, and prudent, he nevertheless often came to decisions more by intuition than by logic. But his self-possession in turmoil marked him out as a born leader. For two years at the Roman College, the multinational seminary founded by St. Ignatius, he had deputized as professor of mathematics for Christopher Clavius, a leading scientist of his day and the principal architect of the new Gregorian calendar. In this post he had acquitted himself with sufficient acclaim to be marked out as Clavius's successor, should the latter not recover from the illness that had forced him to retire temporarily. Another professor, Robert Bellarmine, gave him the sobriquet "pecorella," or little sheep, not to suggest any lack of initiative in him, but simply as a term of endearment.

---

[7] *Spiritual Exercises and Devotions,* 107.

With a talent for mathematics went a love of music. The words Southwell used when he dedicated to a cousin a book of poems might just as well have been addressed to him: "I send you these new ditties; add you the tunes."[8] He was a large-hearted man incapable of anything petty or pusillanimous. These were qualities Southwell especially admired, and he found them in a remarkable degree in his companion.

Brian Garnet, Henry's father, had been master of the grammar school at Heanor near Nottingham. He had sent his son to be educated at Winchester, a school that on several occasions had manifested its reluctance to accept the change of religion. Devotion to our Lady had characterized its scholars from the time of its endowment by William of Wykeham in 1378 and would explain why Garnet also was now anxious to visit Loreto. He had not, like other scholars, gone from school to New College, Oxford, but had instead worked for a year in a London printer's office before following his distinguished Wykamist predecessors—Thomas Stapleton, Nicholas Sanders, John Rastell, and Thomas Harding—to the seminary at Douai.

Although he was six years older than Southwell, both had received their early Jesuit training at Sant'-Andrea under the same novice master, Fabio de Fabiis, one of the most eminent Jesuits of the time. To the end of their lives, both men revered him as a saint: he was the last of the distinguished Roman family that traced its descent from Quintus Fabius Cunctator, who had fought Hannibal to a stalemate in the Second Punic War.

Two months after Garnet had entered Sant'Andrea, another Englishman, William Weston, from King's School, Canterbury, had followed him into the

---

[8] *Poems,* 2.

noviceship. Weston was now in England nervously
awaiting the arrival of the two young Jesuits. Later
referring back to their days together in Rome, he was
to testify to Garnet's capacity for friendship. "There
was never a man," he wrote, "to whom I was more
closely united in the bonds of peace and friendship."
And he explained that "in the same city, at the same
time, in the same house of Sant'Andrea, under the
same teacher, we had set before us the same ideals we
share in common today."[9] They were the ideals Garnet
shared also with Southwell.

From Ancona the two priests rode north via
Modena, Parma, and Piacenza to Milan. This may have
been the route taken by Southwell six years earlier, but
in the reverse direction, when he had walked from
Paris to Rome. He had done this to prove his man-
hood. On deciding that the vocation of a Carthusian
monk was not for him, he had sought admission to the
Society of Jesus at Tournai in 1578, but he had repeat-
edly been turned down: he was considered too imma-
ture and was told to wait. He felt this more sorely because his most intimate friend, John Deckers, had at
the same time been accepted by the Flemish Jesuits.
The two had studied together at Douai at the Jesuit
college of Anchin, where they had attended the lectures
of Leonard Lessius, a young professor who was on
terms of comradeship with his pupils. Lessius, a brilliant ascetical theologian as well as a Scripture scholar,
had been their confessor and confidant and had perhaps determined their vocation. Now traveling north,
Southwell was looking forward with increasing pleasure
to his reunion with Deckers before crossing to England.

---

[9] W.W. to Oliver Manares (March 27, 1598), Stonyhurst:
Anglia, 2, 34; see W.W., 250.

At Milan Garnet and Southwell were joined by a Flemish Brother, William, who had been detailed to act as their guide, servant, and interpreter and to arrange their passage to England. Between Milan and the Alps, Southwell became concerned for their horses. "The sore on William's mount is not yet healed," he told the rector of the English College in Rome, "and I am afraid for the chestnut, too, which has been galled by the baggage since we left Loreto."[10] Taking his cue as he always did from the circumstances of the moment, Southwell later meditated, "If the carrier hath regard not to load his beast more than he is able to bear, how much more wary is God . . . in not suffering us to be tempted above our force."[11]

In a similar vein, Southwell recalled these days in his *Epistle,* reflecting again that "to the wayfarer wandering in the dark and misty night, every light never so small is comfortable; and to the stranger that travelleth in a land of divers languages any that can, though it be brokenly, speak the country's tongue, doth not a little rejoice him" (3). Southwell could manage perfectly in French but was a stranger to German, which Garnet knew well enough: in Rome Garnet had been a member of an international community, while Southwell for all but a few months had been with his compatriots at the English College.

During the tedious hours on the road, the two priests discussed books and poetry. Later Southwell would write some minor masterpieces of prose and a few enduring poems; Garnet would publish a number of small devotional works. In the letters he sent back to Rome while making his way north, Southwell concealed nothing from his friends. Giant-hearted but young in

---

[10] C.R.S., vol. 5 (May 26, 1586).

[11] *Epistle of Comfort,* 28.

years, he suffered alternating moods of exaltation and depression. Whether exhilarated, alarmed, or apprehensive, he reacted in a deeply personal manner to every experience. Garnet, although in no way volatile, was already becoming dependent on Southwell's affection and advice.

On their arrival in Flanders, they stayed at Douai, Southwell's spiritual nursery, where he met John Deckers, now like himself a Jesuit priest. Their time together was short. From Douai they rode on to St. Omer. The town was ideally situated for embarkation at either Boulogne, Dunkerque, or Calais, all within half a day's journey. From there on July 2, five days after saying good-bye to Deckers, he wrote to his friend a letter betraying his nervousness. Instructions for their sailing had not yet arrived from Rome. "This is most inconvenient," he grumbled, "for we may have to stay here longer than we can remain hid. Meanwhile I beg of you, do not let any English people know where we are or that we have been there until I write to you from the port."[12]

Their presence in Flanders remained undetected, although a spy, Thomas Morgan, resident in Paris, had got word of them. On July 3, the day after Southwell wrote to Deckers, Morgan sent a message for Sir Francis Walsingham, who directed the government intelligence service on the Continent: "There are two Jesuits sent to England," he informed his master, "both very young men. Father Southwell and Father Garnet."[13]

At last on July 15 they received their instructions to prepare to embark the following day. In haste Southwell dispatched his promised letter to Deckers. It was a tense moment in his life. His imagination was

---

[12] For full text see Devlin, 98.

[13] State Papers, Dom. Eliz., vol. 18, no. 21.

fervid. It was the eve of a hazardous enterprise that had long been lodged in his imagination and dreams. He was afraid, but had no thought of pulling back. Echoing the words of Aquaviva, he wrote: "It is true that I am being sent 'among wolves,' and likely enough 'to be led to the slaughter.' I only wish it were 'as a lamb' for his name's sake who sent me. . . . The flesh is weak and can do nothing and even now revolts from what is proposed." Then he steeled himself for the ordeal, recalling St. Paul's words, "He will not fail the challengers who himself has framed the challenge." Earnestly he begged for prayers. "Plead, then, for me, my Father. Perhaps it is the last time I shall address you; plead my cause—it is the cause of the Church— that I who play His part may so sustain it as God Himself, as the Angels, as the Society expects of me, and throw away my life blood, if I must, with fortitude and faith."[14] He had no desire for martyrdom, but he believed in intercessory prayer:

> For the Sun by prayer
> did cease his course and stayed.
> The hungry lions
> fawned upon their prey;
> A walled passage
> through the sea it made.
> From furious fire
> it banished heat away:
> It shut the heavens
> three years from giving rain.
> It opened the heavens
> and clouds poured down again.[15]

Garnet was silent. Perhaps he did not permit himself, as Southwell did, to picture the details of execution that might well await him. The poet in Southwell

---

[14] For full text see Devlin, 99f.

[15] McDonald, 150.

would soon develop a seam of meditation that time and again brought him comfort. God permitted the flesh of martyrs to be mangled only to make it more glorious in the second casting.

> And as the paperer of old rotten shreds, oftentimes gathered out of unclean dunghills, by his industry maketh so fine, white and clean paper that it is apt to receive any curious drawing, painting or limning; so our scattered parts by you cast into dunghills, he will restore to such purity of perfection that they shall be more capable of his glorious ornaments than they were before."[16]

It was expected that they would land on the coast of Norfolk, Southwell's home county, where there were friends to shelter them. A watch was being kept for them there. Instead they decided to make a frontal landing across the Channel, even though in the past years twelve priests had been taken coming ashore on the coasts of Kent and Sussex. Southwell perhaps feared that he would not be safe in Norfolk. For the last six years his father had been a conforming Protestant and was now using a rising young lawyer, Edward Coke, in a crop of family lawsuits, the very man who was later as attorney general to be the chief prosecutor at the trial of both priests.

Before embarking, they recited together the first vespers of the feast of St. Alexis, a fifth-century saint who had died a nameless death in a hospital at Edessa in Mesopotamia. He had lived by begging. At his death it was discovered that he was a Roman patrician. In the Middle Ages he was the subject of a popular epic that must have appealed to Southwell, who "without care of coin" had abandoned all his family could offer to return an outlaw to his own country.

---

[16] *Epistle of Comfort,* 236.

About two in the afternoon they set sail. "The wind was blowing hard against us," Garnet wrote two weeks later in his first letter from England to Claudio Aquaviva, "and we had to use the oars to keep the ship on course. But after sunset the wind changed direction, the sea became calm, and we sailed as gently as if we were on a river."[17] In a fragment of a poem Southwell recaptured these hours at sea:

> The ship that from the port doth sail,
> And lanceth in the tide
> Must many a billow's boisterous brunt
> And stormy blast abide.[18]

The demeanor of the two Fathers impressed the Flemish sailors. They remarked among themselves that they were good men whom God had been pleased to help on their way, for there were freebooters in the Channel whom they were fortunate to escape.

The early contrary winds had upset their plan. They had calculated to land ten hours after raising anchor, so that they could step ashore at midnight on an unguarded stretch of beach. But day was already breaking when they reached the English coast. At a point about a mile east of Folkestone and hidden from the town, the ship's boat was lowered. The Flemish Brother took the oars. As they pulled close to the shore, it was Garnet's turn to be alarmed. On a bluff overhanging the beach, they saw a man eying them intently, apparently suspicious that they should be coming ashore at a place such a distance from the harbor. "The sight filled us with foreboding," wrote Garnet.

---

[17] H.G. to C.A. (July 30, 1586), F.G. 651.

[18] McDonald, 159.

Nevertheless they landed.[19] The Brother carried them ashore on his shoulders so that they could step dryshod onto the sand.[20] He then waded back to the cockboat.

"The die was cast," Garnet wrote. Then he comforted himself with the reflection that the fate awaiting them, whatever it might be, "did not hang on the blind forces of darkness, but on the provident disposition of divine providence."

---

[19] H.G. to C.A. (July 30, 1586), F.G. 651.

[20] The only place where the steep cliffs between Folkestone and Dover made a landing possible was about a mile east of Folkestone at a point called the Warren. Behind it was some rising ground, Copt Hill, which would have hidden their landing from the small fishing village of Folkestone.

TWO

THE PROSPECTS . . . BEFORE US

T he trepidation that Garnet experienced when he stepped ashore was still fresh in his mind ten years later, when in a letter to Aquaviva he told the story of his first day in England.

Without loss of nerve Garnet approached the menacing figure on the cliff, cursing the ship's captain who had breached his contract in setting them down at such a distance from the harbor.

The man was no spy, but an honest, kind shepherd who expressed his distress at the imagined injury that had been inflicted on the two priests. Since neither of them was familiar with the countryside, Garnet asked for directions and was given the name of several places in the district. Then the man swore an oath that he had been as truthful with them as he would have been with his own mother and father.

This was their first piece of good fortune. The charm and openness of their character had allayed any emergent suspicion. There was always something in their approach to strangers that quickly won them sympathy.

Garnet remembered every detail of this day. In his letter he recalled, perhaps for the sake of Fr. Clavius, the gap that separated the English from the Gregorian calendar that he had followed on the Continent. "I remember that we said the first Vespers of St Alexis," he wrote, "but on the following morning, as the sun was rising, we landed on the feast of St. Thomas—ten days earlier. Also we were in his diocese between Dover and Folkestone, so we were under his protection, though at the time we did not realize it."[1]

As they walked away from the shore, they made their confession to each other; then, to avoid being arrested together, they separated. They decided to meet again in London.

Garnet quickened his step. He skirted every hamlet in his path, telling himself that an unseen spy might have ridden ahead to raise the alarm in the first populated place he would pass through. During the long, empty days of waiting at St. Omer, he had remained apparently self-possessed while Southwell had betrayed anxiety. Now, separated from Southwell, he discovered his steadiness of nerve deserting him. Southwell was now to show the greater resourcefulness.

"Avoiding the towns on the coast like the plague," Garnet struck inland. He spoke to no one. After he had covered ten miles, he felt hungry and exhausted, but he was still anxious. Deliberately he walked past the inn of the hamlet he happened to be passing and approached a private house. "There with assumed ignorance," he wrote, "I enquired whether or not there was an inn in the place. The answer naturally was that I had just passed it." Feigning simplicity—the device that had saved him earlier in the day—he asked the daughter of the house to give him a drink, for he was too fatigued to retrace his steps. He was invited to

---

[1] H.G. to C.A. (July 30, 1586), F.G. 651. The reference remains the same for the rest of the account of H.G.'s journey to London.

enter, to sit down and answer questions about himself. "So cleverly and cunningly were the questions put," he recalled, "I might have been in a court of law." Then he recalled how St. Paul at Athens, puzzled at first by the persistence of his interrogators, suddenly realized that his hosts were anxious only to gather news which they could retail. The girl was nothing more than curious. After a short time she and her father put Garnet at his ease. Sustaining the role of a traveler unfamiliar with the area, he said he would welcome the chance to return their hospitality should they ever come to London.

There was something, however, in his speech and in the cut of his clothes that almost gave him away. His accent sounded strange in the ears of his Kentish hosts, and there was something distinctly foreign in the cut of his clothes. He was taken first for a Fleming and asked why he was making for London at a time when all stray persons on the road were picked up and sent abroad to the wars in Flanders.

The people of Kent were accustomed to strangers. From the beginning of the reign, Protestant refugees from the Continent had been welcomed there. In a number of towns, French and Flemings had already set up factories for baize, linen, and flannels. After the sack of Antwerp in 1576, there had been a flow of fresh immigrants: by the end of the century Sandwich was to contain more foreigners than natives. It was a calculated policy, backed by acts of Parliament, to repair the economy of the country damaged by the dissolution of the monasteries. Canterbury, which had lived largely on its pilgrim traffic, had suffered severely: twenty-six wagons had been used to remove the treasures from St. Thomas's shrine; the grounds of St. Augustine's had now been turned into a deer park, the Franciscan friary into a cloth factory. Garnet's hosts too were used to the appearance of foreigners. But Garnet was unaware of

this and congratulated himself that he had not pro-
voked any suspicion of his priesthood. He continued his
journey with the words of Moses on his lips: "Fiant
immobiles sicut lapis, donec pertranseat populus tuus,
Domine, populus tuus quem possedisti" (Let them
become immoveable like a stone, O Lord, until thy
people pass by, thy people whom thou hast made thy
possession [Ex. 15:16]).

For his way through Kent on his first day, St.
Thomas protected him. Over many miles all the roads
leading to Canterbury were crowded with people on
their way to St. Thomas's fair; Garnet mingled with
them. "We had St Thomas's protection," he wrote,
"though we did not know it at the time. This was the
reason for our safe journey, the crowds that flocked to
the fair."

Garnet does not say where he passed his first
night ashore. The next morning he took the high road
for the first time; until then he had used the old pilgrim tracks. As he neared Gravesend, the gateway to
the port of London, he was overtaken by a man on
horseback. It was Southwell. They stayed together just
long enough to exchange congratulations that "neither
so far had met with misfortune." Not to be left behind,
Garnet purchased a horse at a nearby farm and
reached Gravesend that evening. From there to the
Tower wharf, there was a regular service of tilt-boats.
Taking the night service, he arrived in London in the
early dawn. "There to my great joy," he told Aquaviva,
"I met my companion in the street. For five or six
hours we walked about the city but failed to find a
friend. Then by chance we came across the man we
were looking for."

In this first report to Rome, Garnet is careful not
to mention Southwell by name: he refers to him always
as his friend or companion or, after Southwell's arrest,

as Robert. Their unidentified guide was no doubt one of Southwell's former students in Rome, who would have been secretly alerted to his coming. This man took them to breakfast in a prison, the one place where they were certain to find fellow Catholics. With the help they received there, they were directed to a safe hiding place, where they remained until William Weston, the only Jesuit then at liberty in England, sought them out. They could hardly have come to London at a more perilous time. At once Weston shepherded them out of the city and thus almost certainly saved them from arrest.

Almost on that very day, the severest persecution yet suffered by English Catholics was now reaching its traumatic climax. In the first six months of the year, seven priests, all from the seminary founded by Cardinal Allen at Douai, had been condemned for their priesthood and executed at Tyburn, York, and on the Isle of Wight. In June, a month before the new priests landed, there had been a systematic clearance of the London prisons to make space available for the men marked out for arrest after the "discovery" of the Babington Plot. Weston, exceptionally farsighted, saw this as a curtain-raiser for the drama of the execution of Mary Queen of Scots, Queen Elizabeth's cousin. Lists of all Catholics in prison were drawn up for Secretary Walsingham, who divided them into three classes: some "most dangerous men" were listed for execution, others for transportation abroad, and the third group, composed of young and active men, for perpetual internment in the castles of Wisbech or Ely in the fen country. By the end of July all the prisons were ready to receive their new intake.[2]

---

[2] H.G., 29. The Babington Plot was a scheme to rescue Mary Queen of Scots, then a prisoner in England. Participating in it, along with Anthony Babington, were a number of young romantic Catholic

Fortune smiled on Garnet and Southwell. A search of all Catholic houses in and about London had been ordered the very day they had embarked at Calais; the day they came ashore, bands of pursuivants or priest hunters were roving the streets of London winckling out all priests in the city. Southwell said that he "met with Catholics first amid swords and then in prison." Thanks to their contact with the prisoners, he and Garnet found fairly sheltered accommodation with an innkeeper.[3]

When seven years earlier Edmund Campion and Robert Persons landed at Dover, there had been rumors of a "Jesuit invasion." The same alarms were repeated now. "News of our coming has already spread abroad," wrote Southwell, "and from the lips of the Queen's Council *my name* has become known to certain persons. The report alarms our enemies, who fear heaven knows what at our hands."[4]

Already Southwell and Garnet had "marvellously cheered and inspirited Catholics," who had heard of their arrival and were showing no fear of the law by offering to shelter them. "So great is our friends' opinion of the Society that we are forced to conceal that we are of it, 'lest the whole of Jerusalem be disturbed.'"[5]

For some days the two priests stayed on at the inn until they were joined by William Weston. Here Weston takes up the story. "Some days after I got back [to London]," he writes, "I was told that two of our Fathers had arrived. . . . So putting everything aside I

---

gentlemen; but government agents infiltrated the group and set the plot in motion in July 1556, representing it as an attempt to assassinate Queen Elizabeth.

[3] R.S. to C.A. (July 25, 1586), C.R.S., 5:307.

[4] Ibid.

[5] H.G. to C.A. (July 30, 1586), F.G. 651.

went at once to the inn where they were staying. . . .
We greeted one another and embraced and dined there
together."[6]

It was in the same place the same day but in
another room that Weston took his farewell of his
friend Anthony Babington, the well-read and adventur-
ous young man of wealth who had been trapped into a
plot woven by Walsingham, the Queen's secretary of
state and spymaster, to bring ruin to the Catholic
cause. Although Babington's only object was to rescue
Mary Queen of Scots, who had been wrongfully imprisoned by her cousin, the plot was skillfully manipulated
by Walsingham, who presented it as an attempt on the
life of the Queen herself.

Southwell and Garnet might well have been arrested that day. With only hours to spare before the
chase closed in on them, the three Jesuits rode out of
London. From St. Giles-in-the-Fields they followed the
Oxford road past Tyburn, and on reaching Brentford
they took the left fork to Hounslow Heath, then
crossed the alluvial meadows of the Colne. Leaving the
Castle of Windsor on their left, they forded the
Thames at Maidenhead, then took a narrow wooded
lane that brought them out again on the Thames at
Hurley, two miles upriver from Marlow and some thirty
miles from London. Here, across the river, was their
refuge, Hurleyford House, on the borders of Buckinghamshire and Berkshire.

This was the seat of Richard Bold, an ardent
musician, from Bold, near Prescot in Lancaster, who
like his neighbor, Richard Shireburn of Stonyhurst,
though a Catholic at heart, had conformed to the new
worship for the sake of expediency. In anticipation of
the priests' arrival, Bold had gathered a number of

---

[6] W.W., 69.

friends to greet them. In the party were Sir George Peckham of Denham, Bold's cousin, and the brother-in-law of John Gerard, a young Jesuit still in training abroad. Also present was William Fitton of Bailes, who at the time was exchanging letters on musical matters with William Byrd.

The freshness, the youth, and the talent of the two priests from Rome caused a stir among the Catholics living in the Thames valley. Weston does not mention by name all who were present at Hurleyford House, but he speaks of William Byrd,

> the very famous musician and organist [who] had been attached to the Queen's chapel, where he had gained a great reputation but had sacrificed everything for the faith—his position, the court, and all those aspirations common to men who seek preferment in royal circles as a means of improving their fortunes.[7]

In this year Byrd was engaged in setting to music the poems contained in his *Psalms, Sonnets and Songs of Sadness and Piety.* The meeting was the beginning of a lifelong friendship between Byrd and Garnet, and it gave Southwell the opportunity of making himself familiar with the new forms of English verse still current only in manuscript, such as the work of Sir Edward Dyer, the poet and courtier, well known to Byrd. It is not difficult to see the influence that some of Dyer's poems, such as "Silence augmenteth grief," an elegy for his close friend, Sir Philip Sydney, exerted on Southwell's poems at this period.

> In eaves, sole sparrow sits not more alone,
> Nor mourning pellican in desert wild:
> Then silly I, that solitary moan,
> From highest hopes to hardest hap exiled.[8]

---

[7] W.W., 71.

[8] *Poems,* 35.

This verse might well have been attributed to Dyer, like much else written in this vein by Southwell.

Although Garnet and Byrd were to meet later, there is no reason to rule out further meetings between Byrd and Southwell, although none is recorded. Also present was William Fitton, like Garnet a musician, for in this year in a nearby Buckinghamshire parish raiders seized a "Popish songbook" and inside its pages found a letter of William Byrd to Fitton.

"Popish songs" would certainly cover Eucharistic hymns. It seems very likely that the gathering of musical talent at Hurleyford House inspired Southwell's translations of Aquinas's verses in honor of the Blessed Sacrament: they have a felicity of phrase unmatched in later versions. Southwell's "A Holy Hymne" is a translation of Aquinas's "Lauda Sion."

> Praise, O Sion, praise thy Saviour,
> Praise thy Captain and thy Pastor
> With hymns and solemn harmony.
> What power affords perform indeed,
> His worth all praises far exceed,
> No praise can reach his dignity.
>
> . . . .
> When the priest the host divideth,
> know that in each part abideth
> All that the whole host covered,
> Form of bread not Christ is broken,
> Not of Christ but of his token
> Is state and stature altered. (23)

But perhaps more successful is his rendering of the ancient hymn "Victimæ paschalis laudes," sung during Holy Week. The subject is the last supper of Christ with his apostles in the cenacle.

> They say, they heard, they felt him sitting
>   near,
> Unseen, unfelt, unheard, they him received,
> No divers thing, so divers it appear,

> Though senses fail, yet faith is not deceived,
> And if the wonder of the work be new,
>   Believe the work because his word is true. (26)

Probably it was Southwell's translations of these hymns that Garnet used later when he arranged for Eucharistic processions in the grounds of Enfield Chase in the early days of the next reign.

In the chapel at Hurleyford House, William Bold had constructed an organ and had trained his family and servants as choristers. Garnet had a fine singing voice and at the daily Mass may well have sung one of Byrd's three Masses, which can be dated to this time as much as to an earlier or later period.

But there was other business to be done at this meeting. William Weston, who had guided his companions out of London, had a premonition that his days of liberty were few. Calling on his two years' experience in England, he outlined to the newcomers the lines on which he proposed their work should develop. "I told them what I knew of conditions in England," he wrote. "Then we discussed our methods of future work and the prospects that lay before us."[9]

In April 1585, just fifteen months earlier, Weston had been at the London house of a leading Catholic peer, Lord Vaux of Harrowden, and had there presided at a conference of Catholic laymen. Its purpose had been to devise countermeasures to the act of Parliament of the previous March aimed at "the utter extirpation of Popery" in England.[10] The act had not only made it treason for any priest born in England and ordained overseas to return to the country, but extended the same penalty of death by hanging, disemboweling, and quartering to all men and women who

---

[9] W.W., 72.

[10] 27. Eliz. cap. 2.

gave shelter to any such priests. "These had been days of immeasurable suffering," Weston recalled later, for the government used every device to harry and hunt down priests and those who sheltered them. "Men lay in ambush for them," he wrote; "others betrayed them, or attacked them with violence. . . . They plundered them at night, confiscated their goods, drove off their flocks, stole their cattle."[11] From that time all priests had been left to shift for themselves in inns and hostels, visiting Catholic homes only at the invitation of their owners. Since in accordance with the government's plans, it could only be a matter of time before virtually all Catholic priests were caught, these laymen gathered under Weston's direction came forward in defiance of the law and at risk of their lives and property to offer sheltered homes from which priests could work.

Now at Hurleyford House, just a year and three months later, the disposition of priests was planned. As more Catholics came forward, the future pattern of the Catholic Church in England was slowly drawn, for these houses became the clandestine churches of the country.

It was left principally to Garnet and Southwell to put the plan into practice. While Garnet was to ride through the shires seeking safe lodgings among the Catholic gentry for incoming priests, Southwell was given the task of setting up a posting station for them in London. Thanks to his years in the English College in Rome, he already knew a large number of students shortly to enter England on completion of their course of studies. Now it became his responsibility to give these young men temporary lodgings in London until they could be directed to the new sheltered centers in the provinces.

---

[11] W.W., 31 and notes.

Until the Hurleyford meeting there had been no organization among the priests working in England. Several counties were altogether without a single priest. As Southwell explained in a letter to Aquaviva, "It is to be regretted that in many counties containing no small number of Catholics there is not even one priest. . . . And worse, the priests actually at work here make for one or two counties leaving others without shepherds."[12]

Before the priests at Hurleyford dispersed, there was to have been a final farewell celebration of the Liturgy. "If all had fallen out as we had wished," wrote Southwell, "we should have sung Mass with all solemnity, accompanied by special instrumental and vocal music, on the feast of St. Mary Magdalene [July 22]. But this, however, was put off to the next day, and as I was called away I could not be present."[13]

---

[12] R.S. to C.A. (July 25, 1586), C.R.S., 5:309.
[13] Ibid.

THREE

HEMMED IN BY DAILY PERILS

Early that morning Southwell rode to London. He had been asked by the Catholics in the Marshalsea Prison to preach to them on the feast of Mary Magdalen. It was an invitation that he would have been particularly pleased to accept, for the saint had often provided matter for his meditations and was shortly to become the subject of two poems. In "Mary Magdalen's Blush" he shares the saint's remorse and tears:

> Bad seed I sowed: worse fruit is now my gain:
> Soon dying mirth began long living pain.
> . . . .
> Remorse doth teach my guilty thoughts to
>   know,
> How cheap I sold that Christ so dearly
>   bought.[1]

Then in a later poem he voices Magdalen's pain at her separation from the passionate object of her love:

> Sith my life from life is parted:
>   Death come take thy portion.
> Who survives, when life is murdered,
>   Lives by mere extortion.

---

[1] *Poems,* 32.

All that live, and not in God:
    Couch their life in death's abode.

Seely stars must needs leave shining,
    When the sun is shadowed.
Borrowed streams refrain their running,
    When head springs are hindered.
One that lives by other's breath,
    Dieth also by his death. (2)

After hearing Southwell's sermon, his congregation begged him for the text, which he later (it seems) expanded into a small book to which he gave the title *Mary Magdalen's Funeral Tears*. Lurking in his distinguished audience was a government spy who reported to his master, Francis Walsingham:

> Among other guests were three gentlewomen two of them daughters of Sir John Arundell. . . . It was Magdalen's day, and the priest catechised the company with the doctrine of popish repentance, taking for his theme the story of Magdalen, absurdly applying the same to his purpose.[2]

It says much for the expectation aroused by Southwell that the two Arundell sisters risked imprisonment to visit Southwell in the Marshalsea. It may have been that they had persuaded him to accept the invitation to preach, for it was to Dorothy, later to become a Benedictine nun in the English convent in Brussels, that he dedicated the *Funeral Tears,* addressing her as the "Worshipful and vertuous Gentlewoman, Mistress D. A. Your vertuous request, to which your desert gave the force of a commandment, won me to satisfy your devotion in penning some little discourse of the Blessed Mary Magdalen."[3]

---

[2] State Papers Elizabeth, Dom. Addenda, 21, no. 97.

[3] Devlin, 117f.

Dorothy was the daughter of Sir John Arundell of Lanherne and had perhaps heard of Southwell from Fr. John Cornelius, who was well known to the family: Cornelius had been sent by Sir John to Rome, where he had studied for the priesthood under Southwell's tuition. His wealth, personal courage, and the splendor of his living had earned him the name of "the great Arundell." If his daughters had been arrested on the occasion of Southwell's sermon, they would have become invaluable pawns in the hands of the government.

Garnet soon followed Southwell to London. From there both priests, without consulting each other, sent their first letters to Aquaviva in Rome, for it was possible only from there to dispatch letters safely to the Continent in the privileged mail of the Spanish Embassy. In his letter Garnet reported briefly their safe arrival and the stir it had caused among Catholics, ending in haste: "I can write no more. . . . It is just that now I want you to know that we are unscathed. It will not be possible to write to my friends, nor will I be able to write to you for some months. Good-bye in the Lord. Keep us in mind. Yours Hen. 30 July 1586."[4]

Southwell, who had written eight days earlier, might well have been caught by this time. Instead, it was Weston that they got. While all three were in London, the Babington Plot was brought to a head. On August 3, just twelve days after the dispersal of the meeting at Hurleyford House, Weston was arrested in the city outside Bishopsgate by two of Walsingham's agents who had been lying there in wait to catch, not Weston, but Anthony Babington himself, who was known to be in hiding in the same district.

---

[4] Ibid., 118.

The relationship between the two priests who had landed together less than a month earlier was now altered. By an instruction of Aquaviva given before they left Rome, Garnet, in the event of Weston's capture, was to succeed him as superior. No longer were they two newcomers acting under an experienced companion, but two friends, the elder of whom was to play a protective and counseling role to his fellow Jesuit.

In his first letter, written five days before Garnet's, Southwell spoke of being "hemmed in by daily perils, never safe even for the briefest moment." The persecution that followed the arrest of Babington was widespread. In spite of additional staff enrolled to help the peace, the county sessions were unable to draw up the indictments of recusants brought before them. The populace was ready to believe any mad story of attempted regicide. There was rumor that a general massacre of Catholics was being planned. Catholics would leave their homes and pass the autumn in fields outside the city or would hire boats and paddle up and down the river until dawn.

For the space of six weeks, from his cell in the Tower, Weston saw Catholics, many of whom he knew personally, being ferried up the river for trial, bound hand and foot. "It was easy to pick them out," he wrote, "from all the other river passengers by the uniform of their guards and the crowds that took off in light boats to follow them the entire stretch of the river to mock or to console them."[5]

When Garnet nearly a year later had an opportunity of writing again to Aquaviva, he was full of admiration of Southwell's behavior the previous autumn. In fact, Southwell seemed to have led a charmed life. On landing in England he appears not to have expected

---

[5] W.W., 83.

more than a few months of freedom. Now he had experienced two almost miraculous escapes. Garnet tells the story of the first in a few sentences:

> A traitor had caught sight of our Robert and instead of immediately pouncing on him, he followed him for a long distance in order to track him down to the house for which he was making and there make a bigger haul. But Robert, who likes to walk at a brisk pace, though unaware that he was being shadowed by a spy, suddenly hastened his stride and vanished altogether from the man's sight. Therefore there was no flattering reward for the traitor when he got back to Walsingham but only harsh words instead.[6]

Although Southwell escaped, the houses of William Byrd and Francis Brown, who had been with him at Hurleyford, were searched. Hurleyford House itself was raided and Richard Bold taken to prison. As Southwell wrote,

> All highways were watched, infinite houses searched, hue and cry raised, scares bruited in people's ears as though the whole realm had been on fire, whereas in truth it was but the hissing of a few green twigs of their own kindling which without any such uproar they might have quenched with a handful of water.[7]

On leaving London after the dispatch of his first letter, Garnet had ridden north to the home of Eleanor Brooksby, the eldest of Lord Vaux's three daughters, at Shoby in Leicestershire, one of the midland counties in greatest need of priests.[8] Southwell at the same time

---

[6] H.G. to C.A. (March 17, 1593). Stonyhurst: Anglia 1, 73.

[7] *Humble Supplication,* 22.

[8] The manor house, partly rebuilt and now called the Priory Farm, stands today. At the front is a line of mullioned windows, where watch could be kept for pursuivants; behind the two old fireplaces Mass vestments are said to have been found; and adjoining the kitchen in the rear is an old, partly ruined building called the

had made his home in Hackney at Vaux's London house. Thus the Vaux family became the means of implementing the first stage of the plan worked out at Hurleyford with William Weston.

By marriage Garnet's hostess was connected with the Gatesbys, Treshams, and Throckmortons. Working with these families, Garnet was able to slowly build up what another Jesuit was to call "the churches in those parts." In the course of the next twenty years, he was able to set up a network of closely linked and strategically spaced Catholic centers throughout the southern midlands.

Both Garnet's and Southwell's movements had been carefully watched. On November 4 Anthony Tyrrell, a renegade priest whose sleuthing for the government had not yet been detected, received information that Southwell was residing at Vaux's Hackney House. The next day London's chief magistrate, Richard Young, took the unusual step of leading the search for him in person, an indication perhaps of the fame attaching to his name only four months after his coming to England. Young chose the early morning for the raid, when he was likely to surprise Southwell at Mass. Vaux's doorkeeper resisted the searchers just long enough to allow Southwell time to hide. "The pursuivants were rampaging all round the house," he wrote to Aquaviva the following December 21. "I heard them shouting and breaking down the woodwork and sounding the walls in search of hiding places. But after a few hours, thanks to God's goodness, they failed to find me although there was only a thin partition and not a wall that separated me from them." For several days afterwards the house was

chapel. See G. Anstruther, *Vaux of Harrowden* (1953), 389.

watched, and Southwell was "forced for several nights to sleep in his clothes in a very strait and uncomfortable place.[9]

In his haste to hide, Southwell had left some papers lying in his room. Among them were two of his own letters signed Robertus, which led to a false report that Robert Persons was back in England.

It was the same informant or possibly the discovery of other papers in the course of the search that led to a break-in at Shoby about the same time. On this occasion the raiders were foiled by Mrs. Brooksby's adopted daughter, Frances Burroughs, then aged eleven: "Her courage was such that she was never daunted or afraid of anything."

As at Hackney the searchers broke in at dawn, Garnet was at Mass in the room above the hall, where another priest was also present. On hearing the disturbance below, Eleanor with her sister Anne and the young Frances Burroughs came down to meet the constables. Frances took the initiative. "Put up your swords," she commanded, "or my mother will die. She cannot endure the sight of a naked blade." Then turning to fetch some wine for her, she ran upstairs, made fast the door of the hiding place behind the priests, and returned to parley with the servants. On another occasion, possibly in the same year, she barred the staircase after a sudden intrusion. A pursuivant, to frighten her, held a drawn dagger at her breast, threatening to stab her if she refused to hand over the priests. With composure Frances retorted, "If thou dost, it will be the hottest blood that ever thou sheddest in thy life."[10]

The climax of the Babington persecution came on February 8, 1587, with the execution of Mary Queen of

---

[9] R.S. to C.A. (December 21, 1586). C.R.S., 5:311.

[10] Adam Hamilton, *Chronicle of St. Monica's* (1906), 2:165f.

Scots at Fotheringay Castle. Southwell, like the Catholic body, considered her a martyr whose death obliterated in the eyes of God her past failings. True to the instructions they received, neither he nor Garnet made mention of the execution in their letters abroad. Nevertheless, without mentioning her by name, Southwell was inspired to write a poem which can only refer to her. It is the deceased queen who speaks:

> Some things more perfect are in their decay,
> Like spark that going out gives clearest light,
> Such was my hap whose doleful dying day
> began my joy and termed Fortune's spite.
>
> Alive a Queen, now dead I am a saint,
> Once Mary called, my name now martyr is,
> From earthly reign debarred by restraint,
> In lieu whereof I reign in heavenly bliss.
> . . . .
> My scaffold was my bed where ease I found,
> The block a pillow of eternal rest,
> My headman cast me in blissful swound,
> His axe cut off my cares from combered brest.
>
> Rue not my death, rejoice at my repose,
> It was no death to me but to my woe,
> The bud was opened to let out the rose,
> The chains unlosed to let the captive go.
> A prince by birth, a prisoner by mishap,
> From crown to cross, from throne to thrall I
>   fell,
> My right, my ruth, my titles wrought my trap,
> My weal my woe, my worldly heaven my hell.[11]

After narrowly escaping arrest at Hackney, Southwell saw clearly that he must find a refuge where he would be unknown and undisturbed. He was anxious also to live in the city center in a place that would have

---

[11] *Poems,* 47.

at least temporary accommodation for incoming priests. While he was searching for such a refugee, a lady touched him on the sleeve and handed him a message. It was from Anne, countess of Arundel, requesting him to visit her.

His new home was at Arundel House in the Strand, a palatial building that stood in three and a half acres and had the advantage of a river frontage. There, before his imprisonment in the Tower two years earlier, the earl had staged a tourney for the entertainment of the Queen and the French envoys commissioned to arrange for her marriage with the duke of Anjou. Now in a remote part of the palace with its own exit to the river, Southwell developed his nocturnal apostolate, for he did not dare be seen coming and going during the daylight hours. The rest of the building was occupied partly by the lords William and Thomas Howard, Anne's brothers-in-law, and by the government. His earliest biographer explains that Southwell, owing to the number of persons and their attendants resident in the place, was "unable to set foot outside his room or to take the air, even at the window, unless from afar or to share his meals with anyone, or to eat anything except remnants secretly brought him by Catholics or by a few servants of proved fidelity." Only in disguise under cover of night could he venture out. But his day hours were given mainly to prayer, to writing letters, and to literary work.

It was probably in the same month that Mary Queen of Scots was executed that Garnet sought out Southwell for the first of the semiannual meetings that were to be held regularly as the number of Jesuits working in England increased. At this first reunion the two priests carried through a project they had discussed while riding north together from Rome: it was to set up a printing press despite the death penalty for all concerned with it should it be discovered. At the time printing could be undertaken only with a royal license.

We have no precise knowledge about the press or its location, but we have evidence that it was in operation somewhere in the outskirts of the city soon after Garnet's visit.

With his passionate desire to champion the cause of justice, Southwell had written to Aquaviva on January 12 of that year, expressing his dismay at the dissemination of anti-Catholic literature. He had seen that its effect was cumulative, that lies had to be bolstered up by further lies: "What they achieve by lies" he wrote, "they will perforce establish and confirm by lies."[12] Impatiently he had awaited Garnet's visit to find means of combating the spate of pamphlets, tracts, and broadsheets written against the papacy.

It was barely ten years since Garnet had left the employment of the printer Tottel, whose assistant was Whalley, a name that Garnet now assumed after Whalley had moved out of London to set up his own press.

While Southwell moved secretly among the prisoners in the jails of London, Garnet established his own lodgings in the capital, moving frequently as the pursuit for him grew hotter, taking his press from one rented house to another. All the same, within about a year after their arrival, the two priests were using to the full the faculties given them to publish books without reference to Rome and without mention of the true place of production. Only after the press had been in operation for ten years did Garnet dare to mention it in a letter to Rome. Writing on April 16, 1596, he assessed its achievements: "We equipped at our expense a press which in a short space of time filled the kingdom from end to end with catechisms and other books

---

[12] R.S. to C.A. (January 12, 1587), F.G. 651.

of devotion." When it was seized a few months before this letter was written, "a large stock of many divers books was taken."[13] Garnet, however, anxious quickly to make good the loss, maintained his employees on working wages until he could establish another press.

---

[13] H.G. to C.A. (April 16, 1596), Stonyhurst: Anglia 2, 16.

FOUR

OUR LIVES . . . ON A THREAD

I n London Southwell had set up a receiving center for priests entering the country, many of whom he had known in Rome. Thomas Pormont, a Lincolnshire man and a graduate of Trinity, Cambridge, who had been at the English College with him, was one of many he helped in their first weeks in London. There Southwell fed, clothed, and housed him and eventually found him lodgings with a haberdasher in the parish of St. Gregory's near St. Paul's, where two years later he was martyred in the churchyard.

Meanwhile, in the country Garnet was adding every month to the number of houses to which incoming priests could be sent. In fact, by the end of their first year the two young Jesuits had already done much to strengthen Catholicism in England. In a letter of April 16, 1596, Garnet surveys their success:

> When the priests first arrive from the seminaries we give them every help we can. The greater number of them, as opportunity occurs, we place in fixed residences. . . . The result is that very many persons who barely saw a seminary priest once a year, now have one all the time and most eagerly welcome others no matter where they come from.[1]

---

[1] H.G. to C.A. (April 16, 1596), Stonyhurst: Anglia, 2, 16.

Hitherto priests entering England had to shift for themselves and were frequently picked up by pursuivants before they could find a refuge: after landing they had drifted for the most part to London, the only city where accent or lack of connections did not betray them as foreigners. There they had lived precariously in taverns. Often they had been without means of support. Even now, for a period of a few months, the number of priests outstripped the houses to which they could be sent.

Already there was something desperate and defiant in the actions of both Southwell and Garnet. Campion had enjoyed thirteen months of freedom, Weston two years. Southwell's letters become almost feverish: "Our lives hang in the balance; we are not safe but not unduly nervous," and again, "They may put it out as often as they like that I am taken, but I shall endeavour as long as I escape their hands to let them know by my actions that I am still at liberty."[2]

It may have been Southwell's constant appearances among the Catholic prisoners in London that started rumors of his arrest, or it may have been a report deliberately circulated by the government to dispirit his friends; but whatever the case, it gave Garnet many days of anxiety. From their first hours in England, they had depended on each other for inspiration and success; their zeal was well matched, though Southwell's was more vehemently expressed. Garnet had taken a calculated risk in placing him in London, but he knew that if Catholics in the capital recovered their shattered hopes, then the effect would be felt throughout the kingdom. Nevertheless, it was a daring decision when Southwell was in the triumphant mood that comes through these letters. "I am

---

[2] R.S. to C.A. (December 21, 1586), C.R.S., 5:314.

determined," he wrote, after he had twice narrowly escaped arrest, "never to desist from the works of my calling, though the works, when done, cannot long escape their notice and will make them aware that there still lives one of this sort whom they have not yet taken."[3]

On the brink of his departure for England, while waiting to embark at Boulogne, Southwell had almost lost his nerve. Now he was exhilarated by the results of his apostolate. Faced with danger, he showed a spirit of steel. London had found in him a true champion of "religion."

In March he wrote the first pages of his *Epistle of Comfort.* Starting with the letters he sent to Philip Howard, his protector and Anne's imprisoned husband, from which he hoped he would "glean some ears of comfort and pick some few crumbs" for his spiritual repast, he expanded his message for the benefit of all Catholic sufferers. His mood of exultant confidence, apparent from the first page to the last, must have recalled Campion's *Challenge to the Privy Council* of ten years earlier.

The *Epistle* was completed before the end of 1587. In it he takes up the theme of suffering and transfiguration where he left off in *Mary Magdalen's Funeral Tears.* "Our bodies," he writes,

> shall at the resurrection be of most comely and gracious feature, beauteous and lovely, healthful without all weakness, always in the youth, prime and flower of their force, personable in shape, as nimble as our thought, subject to no penal impression, incapable of grief, as clear as crystal, as bright as the sun, and as able to find passage through heaven, earth and any other material stop as is the liquid and yielding air.

---

[3] Ibid.

The transfiguration extends to the mind and heart of love, for then "it shall be lawful to love whatsoever we like, and whatsoever we love we shall perfectly enjoy, and not only love but be also loved as much as we ourselves will desire."[4]

Under pressure of missionary life, Southwell began now to cast off the conceits of his stylized Roman writings. The old precocities of phrase give way to more direct speech; the sustained metaphors remain but with more immediate impact. For the greater part, the book develops the grounds of comfort and sets out the triumphs that await the perseverance of prisoners in their conflict. Suffering is presented as the highest privilege and the surpassing experience of the true Christian. Throughout, Southwell is topical and poetical by turn, devotional and polemical, severe but comforting, while steeling himself for his own trials ahead. Occasionally he draws on his own experience when writing, for example, of the hospitals of Rome when he worked there as a Jesuit novice. "Do but cast your eyes into one hospital of lazars," he writes; "see the cankers, fistulas, ulcers and rottings, the boils, sores and festered carbuncles. . . . Consider the diseases of the eyes, ears, mouth, throat and every parcel of man's body" (69). And from the Roman hospitals he turns to the furnishings of the great houses that flanked Arundel House. The born countryman comes out in countless pages and in his interest in animals also, stimulated partly by the zoo then housed in the Tower of London and partly by a popular work published in 1567, *A Greene Forest, or Naturall Historie* by John Maplet, a source from which Shakespeare later drew

---

[4] *Epistle of Comfort,* 222. Southwell gives no date of publication, but he makes no reference to contemporary events later than 1587. He mentions several English martyrs but none who suffered in 1588, the worst year of persecution.

his information about the behavior of animals. There are long passages that look like a poet's notebook with images and metaphors that are to be found again in his poems and would without doubt have been used in his sermons.

Every chapter of the *Epistle* is a panegyric of the Catholic spirit. The message is one of hope, since the enemies of the Church, no matter how they may strive to suffocate her, are in fact making her future secure by creating "saints enough to furnish all our churches with treasure when it shall please God to restore them to their true honours" (247). Chapter after chapter gives more compelling motives for endurance drawn from philosophy, history, and the situation he had found in England; and these motives are supported by themes from theology and mystical prayer. Denigrated as his fellow Catholics were, Southwell insisted that truth was on their side. "Our adversaries are so fully persuaded of our good behaviour that if a man in company be modest and grave in countenance, words and demeanour, if he used no swearing, foul or unseemly speech, he is straighway suspected for a Papist" (108).

In spite of the persecution that grew more systematic as the danger of the Armada from Spain increased, Garnet like Southwell was in high spirits throughout the summer of 1587. In letters to Rome both expressed the same high hopes for the future. Both pleaded independently for more laborers for the harvest, Southwell in images, Garnet in phrases inspired by Scripture. "The number of people in Christ's city is growing daily. . . . So I implore you in the most earnest manner to send us a supply of men as soon as you can." "Truthfully," wrote Southwell to Aquaviva, "no matter how fiercely the storm rages, the bark of Peter sails on. Any number of persons are trying to come aboard her. . . . Priests only are lacking. Some are due to be sent. See that they come at once."[5]

But there were moments when Southwell suffered depressions. Apocalyptically he saw the kingdom of God near at hand. When he prayed for its coming in the Lord's Prayer, he imagined that "the kingdom of this world is in the waning," its ruin begun and the "forerunners of Anti-Christ in the pride of their course." He saw symptoms of decline as he rode through the countryside—hills tired with digging, wearied mines, fountains with less abundance of water, winter with showers insufficient to water the earth, the summer sun too feeble to ripen the corn; he saw grey heads in children, hair falling out before it was fully grown. "Finally," he reflected, "everything is so impaired and so fast falleth away that happy he may seem that dieth quickly, lest he be oppressed with the ruins of a dying world."[6]

Garnet was again in London in August 1587, presumably on business connected with his press or with the lease of a new house. As usual he took the opportunity it gave him to dispatch a letter to Aquaviva. Already packed and ready to take the road north, by chance he ran into Southwell in the street. "Only yesterday," he wrote again a few days later, "I met Robert altogether by accident. He was reading your Lordship's letter. I am incapable of telling you what joy this gave me."[7] The General's letter was full of praise, affection, and encouragement. He begged Southwell to write to him personally as often as he was able, and he did not forget a message of consolation for William Weston, who was in prison.

---

[5] R.S. to C.A. (December 21, 1586), C.R.S., 5:314.

[6] *Epistle of Comfort,* 158f.

[7] H.G. to CA. (August 29, 1587), F.G. 651.

Southwell, who might correctly have regarded Aquaviva's letter as confidential, handed it to his superior to read. On his side Garnet with propriety informed the General that he had seen it and thanked him for his very personal interest in a priest who was his closest friend, his confessor, and his only subject at liberty. "I saw from your letter," he wrote, "how concerned you were with our safety and with the progress we are making."[8]

In a state of excitement, Southwell replied at once. The pleasure the letter gave him was shared equally by Garnet. "I cannot express in words," Southwell wrote, "the joy your letter gave me. It was like a longed for star to sailors tossed in a tempest, a timely message to souls suspended in the balance and welcome news of affairs at home to their brothers in exile." After twelve months' toil this was the encouragement both priests needed. "We have now experienced," continued Southwell, "the fatherly affection of the very best of fathers. . . . God has granted us the grace to be kept before your eyes and in your heart, unworthy, far away subjects that we are." He had given "fresh courage to men in battle who were happy to have such a person to spur them on and be their father."[9]

But Aquaviva had added a caution. One of Southwell's early letters had been lost in transit. Aquaviva feared that it might have fallen into the hands of the Council. The General gave them a fresh warning to take care of what they wrote and suggested that they should use a code; for instance, creditors and debtors might stand for persecutors and persecuted, priests could be referred to as merchants, people as merchandise. "The matters you discuss," Aquaviva wrote,

---

[8] Ibid.

[9] R.S. to C.A. (August 28, 1587), F.G. 651.

"should be veiled in allegory, especially if they are of importance."[10] While agreeing to the code which was in fact adopted, Southwell had his reservations about the use of allegory. "Anything written obscurely, enigmatically or figuratively," he pointed out, "is liable to close examination and to perverse interpretations. But be assured that we shall never write a word that might bring into peril anyone but ourselves. The dangers we face, though they could be more numerous, can scarcely be greater. Already our lives hang on a thread."[11]

The dangers both shared in common only brought them still closer to each other. "The love of a mortal friend," Southwell wrote at this time, "not only moves us, but enforces us to love him again, and his perils for us make us eager of perils for him, because thereby both our love to him is best witnessed and his love to us best confirmed."[12] It is a passage in which Southwell gets closest to uncovering the grounds of his deep attachment to Garnet.

While in London Southwell received frequent guidance from Weston, who was kept in prison without trial. Perhaps the authorities feared that at the bar he would reveal facts about the Babington Plot that would seriously embarrass the Council. Besides, he was a figure of veneration among Catholics, an oracle of wisdom with a reputation for sanctity comparable to that of the medieval anchorites. The abstemiousness of his life, his charity, his counsel, leadership, and learning made him a bridge uniting Catholics with their cherished past. "If I spoke with the tongue of Campion," ran a current parody of St. Paul, "and wrote with the

---

[10] C.A. to R.S. Archives S.J., Rome: Galliæ, Epis. Gen., f.46. See C.R.S., 5:319-21.

[11] R.S. to C.A. (August 28, 1587), F.G. 651.

[12] *Epistle of Comfort,* 45.

pen of Persons and led the austere life of Fr. Weston and had not charity, it would avail me nothing."[13] A contemporary stated that Weston was the most consulted man in England. For this reason also he had been kept a prisoner in the Clink on the south bank of the river, where Southwell on his frequent rounds of the prisons was able to communicate with him.

Alter eighteen months in the Clink, Weston was transferred by order of the Council to Wisbech Castle, which had been converted into a concentration camp for priests. Before leaving, Weston obtained from his keeper permission to visit certain friends in London. "The next day I changed my habit for lay clothes and went out," wrote Weston. "First of all I visited Catholics confined in other prisons, both priests and laymen, which on my side as well as theirs was source of great joy and happiness." In company with Weston was John, the keeper of the Clink. Anxious to see Southwell alone, Weston gave his parole to return before nightfall. "You have seen that I can be trusted," he addressed John, "and that I am not the sort of person to betray anyone who has done me a kindness." His keeper accepted his word.[14]

Weston merely states that he had long conversations with his friends. Southwell is more detailed. In his letter recalling the meeting, he shows an almost unbounded esteem for the young veteran priest. "Before his departure," he told Aquaviva,

> Weston was allowed to visit friends and friends were allowed to visit him. He received so many requests to call on Catholics that it would certainly be unbelievable if there were not proof of it. And this very high opinion

[13] Archives of the English College, Valladolid, Seville, 17.B.686.

[14] W.W., 140f.

of his saintliness is indeed his due, for he is a true Isra-
elite, prudent as a serpent and simple as a dove. God
grant that we may follow in his footsteps.[15]

Southwell discussed with Weston a frustrating
problem that faced Garnet as superior. It arose from a
proposal of Southwell's hostess, the countess of Arundel. In disguise she had visited Weston in the Clink,
offering to put down a large sum to obtain his release
from prison and his passage into exile, which she knew
would be acceptable to the Council. Weston argued
with her. "He was not committed to prison for money,
so neither would he be released for money," yet he
would have no difficulty in going free if the Council
spontaneously released him. After the countess's visit,
Weston wrote to Southwell asking him to use every
means he knew to hinder her. Now, a second time, at
their meeting he again pressed his point. A few weeks
later Garnet himself settled the matter. Much as he was
anxious to see Weston go free, it was a course liable to
misinterpretation. "Since he has gained for himself an
eminent and illustrious position he is exposed to the
observation of everybody and it would look shameful
for the shepherd to flee from his flock at such a time
as this."[16]

Weston remained in prison for the rest of the
reign. On January 22, 1588, he was taken from the
Clink under escort on the first part of his journey to
Wisbech. Crowds lined the street to see him, others
followed him to the city boundaries. In two years of
confinement he had become a heroic and emblematic
figure, a meek and suffering servant of his people. As
Garnet foresaw, his influence was unimpaired and his
stature unparalleled in the land when he emerged fif-

[15] R.S. to C.A. (January 22, 1588), F.G. 651.

[16] H.G. to C.A. (October 29, 1588), F.G. 651.

teen years later, a blind and broken man, no more than middle-aged, on the Tower wharf, to embark for exile on the Continent in May 1603.

It must have been a difficult decision for Garnet, for Weston still lay under threat of execution. "It was not that I did not shudder at the thought of death," writes Weston, explaining his own feelings, "or that I did not desire to be free. I was very much afraid and I would have welcomed my liberty gladly and with open arms"; but when his companions and a score of seminary priests were daily risking their lives, he did not wish to avail himself of the countess's offer.[17]

Garnet says little of his work between February and July 1588. It was at this time that he decided to move his quarters from the center of the city to its outskirts. Any central residence was liable to periodic inquiries about its occupants and whether or not they "went to church." Eventually Garnet rented a place in Finsbury Fields, probably before midsummer 1588.

It is this house that he describes in a letter of 1593. "Many of the citizens of London," he explained to Aquaviva, "own small gardens beyond the city walls, and a number have built in these gardens cottages to which they resort from time to time to enjoy the cleaner air." The garden cottage that Garnet acquired was divided conveniently into three rooms, a kitchen and dining room on the ground floor, and above a chapel which probably served as sleeping quarters.

> Our priests coming to town on business as well as those living permanently in London usually visited it. Since it was believed that no one was actually residing here, it was never molested by the officers whose duties it is to make the rounds of every house to enquire whether the

[17] W.W., 119.

occupants are in the habit of attending the heretical church.

For greater security Garnet instructed all using the house not to speak even in "a natural voice for fear of being overheard in the road nearby. Nor was it possible in the daytime to prepare food or to light a fire even in the most bitter winter weather, in case the smoke might be seen. All food was cooked by night and eaten cold the next day."[18]

It was here that Garnet and Southwell met to coordinate their work. Here also that Garnet lived when he sent Southwell into the country to organize more stations to which priests might be sent. The garden cottage was put at the disposal of all whom Garnet felt he could trust. In the cellar a cunningly constructed hiding place lay behind an untidy store of beer barrels, logs, and coal. Dark and disorderly, it could conceal six or seven men.

It was to give Southwell relief from the strain of life in the capital that Garnet took his place in London during the autumn of 1588.

---

[18] See H.G. to C.A. (May 15, 1593), F.G. 651, and H.G. to C.A. (March 17, 1593), Archives S.J., Rome: Anglia, I, II, f. 27.

FIVE

To All
What Each One Needed

I n the late summer or early autumn of that year, Southwell again experienced a depression of spirit. He had lost several priest friends in the fury of persecution that heralded and followed the Spanish Armada. He unburdened himself to Aquaviva:

> The storms the heretics stir up every now and again are much worse, and worst of all is that winter in the soul which we must at all costs avoid. By your prayers, Father, we hope to drive it off and that springtime will again return with the flowers coming to bloom and our vineyards breathing forth their fragrance.[1]

In November Garnet wrote that "Robert has gone journeying in order to breathe in a more wholesome climate."[2] He was away for more than seven weeks and rode through a "great part of England." The worst of the persecution was over by October. "I am off on my journeying," Southwell wrote, "caring nothing for foul weather. . . . Sometimes our little ship is tossed up and down on the most fearful waves and at other times when the storm has blown itself out she sits smiling on a quiet sea."[3] The "horrid cruelty," as he calls it, had

---

[1] R.S. to C.A. (December 28, 1588), F.G. 651.

[2] H.G. to C.A. (November 24, 1588), F.G. 651.

[3] R.S. to C.A. (December 28, 1588), F.G. 651.

taken from him two of his closest friends, Christopher Buxton and Edward Jones, executed at Canterbury and at Chichester on October 1.

Riding now through the southern shires, he met his cousins, some young poets, and numerous friends. To lift his depression he reflected indirectly on his personal success:

> Persons who until now would not even speak to a priest, much less admit one into their home, not only take us in but press us to come again or to stay. . . . In most of them I have found a wonderful enthusiasm and a contempt for the values of this world. Men of noble families, with great possessions, surrounded though they are with every privilege, are more and more prepared to put at risk everything they possess including their estates and their liberty.[4]

Escorted from house to house, he found or made friends everywhere. "Many, the sons and heirs of great persons in the land," he wrote, "have been ready to give me not only their companionship but their personal service." It seems that wherever he went he cut the figure of a young gallant at ease in every kind of company. "I have sometimes been to call on Protestant sheriffs in order to care for secret Catholics in their households, and they, observing my fine clothes and my bevy of aristocratic youths, have received me with imposing ceremony and truly sumptuous banquets."[5] It may well have been on a tour like this that he enjoyed the partridge which he mentioned in a letter to Philip Howard. "Though the hawks," he wrote,

> while they are alive are highly prized, daintily fed and honoured upon great persons' fists, yet when they are once dead their bodies serve for nothing but to be

---

[4] Ibid.

[5] *Epistle of Comfort,* 236.

thrown onto the dunghill. The partridge however, whose flesh had been torn with the hawk's talons, is not withstanding served on a silver plate at the king's own table.[6]

In his absence from London, Southwell missed the service at St. Paul's in thanksgiving for the defeat of the Spanish Armada. Garnet, who was still in town, obtained a window seat in the house of a friend on Ludgate Hill that gave him a view of the Queen's reception on the steps of the cathedral. The description of the procession that he gave to Aquaviva, the fullest of its kind by a private onlooker, reveals his genuine happiness at the demonstration of loyalty to the Queen and his hope that the scattering of the Spanish fleet might remove the political ground for continued persecution. Certain features of the pageant, the first of its kind in London since the coronation, appeared to him slightly ludicrous. "On 24 November," he writes,

> this year a solemn procession, or perhaps I should call it a pageant, was held to give thanks to God for scattering the Spanish fleet. It was led by noblemen of the Queen's household mounted on horses caparisoned beyond my powers of description. . . . Behind them rode the Queen's Councillors, and among them all the bishops conspicuous in their square caps and rochets; then the Queen herself, escorted by her ladies-in-waiting, and followed by the principal ladies of the realm all mounted in the same manner.[7]

> The Queen was borne in a gilded chair, which was covered by a canopy high above her head: it hung down behind but was open in front and at the sides. She was drawn by two greys royally caparisoned. The unceasing uproar echoed all round her.

---

[6] Ibid.

[7] For the description that follows, see H.G. to C.A. (December 5, 1588), F.G. 651, no. 7.

Here was an opportunity for Garnet to write about the Queen without transgressing Aquaviva's injunctions. He used it to the full, inserting here and there a wry comment.

> With all this pomp the Queen came forth from Somerset Palace and processed to the great cathedral of St Paul's. When she reached the Temple Bar—it marks the limits of the city and it is here that its jurisdiction begins—she was welcomed by the Lord Mayor and aldermen. Here also she was presented with the sword that is carried before the Lord Mayor only when he is in the presence of the sovereign.
>
> As she continued on her way to St Paul's she was acclaimed by members of the legal profession . . . by representative merchants and craftsmen from the guilds, all seated on bedecked tiers all along the route.
>
> The clergy then came forward to greet her. They looked ill at ease, got up as they were in copes which until now had ordinarily been burnt or torn up or used for profane purposes: they had been fetched in a rather neglected state from the Queen's chapel and from a disused armory in the Tower. . . .
>
> Entering the cathedral the Queen knelt and prayed. Then they all continued on to the place where the high altar used to stand and remained there while the service was conducted. Many of them took communion. Whether they were fasting or not I cannot say: it was almost midday. Afterwards the Queen went to the cross in the churchyard where sermons are usually given. She sat on a raised platform and from time to time applauded the preacher in a loud voice whenever he was praising the Queen's clemency or stating that her aim above all others was to bring peace to the realm.
>
> A banquet was then given by the Bishop of London.[8] After it they processed home by the way they had come. It was shortly before dusk.

---

[8] John Aylmer, bishop of London 1577-94, formerly tutor to Lady Jane Grey and author of several devotional works.

The pageant had been a long time in preparation. There was a rumour that the Queen was reluctant to appear in public. Orders had gone out that no one was to be at a window while she was passing unless the householder was prepared to stake his life and entire fortune on his trustworthiness. There were, however, persons who vouched for me for they believe that I have the Queen's safety more at heart than have her own Calvinistic ministers.

Garnet had already visited his brother and sisters in Nottinghamshire: they had all remained firm in their allegiance to the Church in which they were baptized, and his two sisters were shortly to go overseas to become nuns; his nephew Thomas, who was martyred on June 23, 1608, and canonized in October 1970, was already at the school founded by Robert Persons at Eu and soon to be moved to St. Omer. Of his more extended family nothing is known.

By contrast, through his mother Bridget, Southwell had numerous Copley cousins and connections and could claim kinship with Sir John Coke, Francis Bacon, and William Cecil—all actors in the drama of his brief years in England. The fortunes of his father were well established, but Robert's concern was with his lapse from religious practice. In a letter that leaves regrets that Southwell did not remain on the Continent to assist Gregory Martin in the translation of the Douai Bible, he pleaded with him to return to the faith of his family. The grave beauty of his prose flows from the fear that his father was approaching his death unprepared. "Now therefore," he writes,

> to join issue and to come to the principal drift of my discourse: most humbly and earnestly I am to beseech you, that both in respect of the honour of God, your duty to his Church, the comfort of your children and the redress of your own soul—you would seriously consider

the terms you stand in and weigh yourself in a Christian
balance, taking for your counterpoise the judgements
of God.[9]

His father's health was failing, and his son urged
him

now in the cool and calm of the evening to retire to a
Christian rest and close up the day of your life with a
clear sunset; that having all darkness behind you and
carrying in your conscience the light of grace you may
escape the horror of eternal night and pass from a
mortal day to an everlasting morrow.

The letter is a masterpiece of English prose.
"Good Sir," he added "make no delay. Though you
suffered the bud to be blasted and the flower to fade;
. . . yea, though you let the boughs wither and the body
of your tree to grow to decay; yet, alas! keep life in the
root for fear lest the whole become fuel for hell-fire."
Although enfeebled, Southwell's father had yet some
years left to him. Pleading not only his own but "the
earnest desire of your other children," Southwell spoke
bluntly. "Death," he told his father, "hath already filed
from you the better part of your natural forces. . . . For
what is age but the kalends of death? And what importeth your present weakness but an earnest of your
approaching dissolution?" He should now place himself
on his deathbed and feel the cramps of death wresting
his heartstrings.

Words, phrases, and figures follow hard on one
another, matching the flow of his contemporary and
probable acquaintance, the young William Shakespeare,
who was well known to Southwell's Copley cousins. But
after long pleading his filial sorrow forces him to warn
his father that "custom soon groweth to a second

---

[9] For R.S.'s letter to his father, see *The Triumphs over Death,*
ed. J. W. Trotman (London, 1914), 36-64.

nature and being once full owner of the mind, it can hardly be cast out of possession."[10]

With so many of his young friends suffering execution on the scaffold in the space of ten months, Southwell's poetic mind frequently turned to the theme of death. The poem "Life Is But Losse" is just one example:

> By force I live, in will I wish to die,
>   In plaint I pass the length of lingering days.
> Free would my soul from mortal body fly,
>   And tread the track of death's desired ways;
> Life is but loss where death is deemed gain,
> And loathed pleasures breed displeasing pain.
>
> . . . .
>
> Come cruel death, why lingerest thou so long,
> What doth withold thy dint from fatal stroke?
> Now pressed I am, Alas thou doest me wrong
> To let me live more anger to provoke:
> Thy right is had, when thou hast stopped my
>   breath,
> Why shouldst thou stay, to work my double
>   death?[11]

Undoubtedly part of Southwell's purpose in his journeying was to restore the confidence of his friends in the Catholic cause after the disaster of the Armada. His first concern everywhere was again for the Catholics who had been herded into prisons throughout the country before the Spanish fleet had left harbor. "I was able to do a great deal of work for prisoners and managed to help and console them if they were not in

---

[10] Although the date given in his letter to his father is October 22, 1589, it is likely that it is a revised form of a shorter letter written the year before when his father was compelled to sell Horsham St. Faith to meet the demands of his debtors. See ibid., 88f.

[11] *Poems,* 50.

too strict confinement." He was referring in this letter to the recently established prisons at Ely, Framlingham, and Wisbech, none more than a day's ride from his ancestral home. But at the same time and probably in the same area, he would call at the houses of the gentry to whom his family was known. In an almost Pauline passage, he speaks of himself as striving his utmost to strengthen the weak and wavering, spur on the fervent to even greater efforts, rebuke those who were giving bad example, and, in his own phrase "be to all what each one needed, a father, a shepherd or a judge."[12]

There was never a time when he was not gathering material for his sermons or his poems, noting accurately the conversation, manners, mood, and behavior of those with whom he mixed in the houses of the nobility; observing now a courting gallant at a banquet

> who hath no greater felicity than to do that which may be acceptable to his paramour. . . . Every peril undertaken for her seems pleasant, every reproach honourable, all drudgery delightsome. . . . Her colours seem the fairest, the meat that fitteth her taste sweetest, the fashion agreeable to her fancy seemeth the comeliest. Her faults are virtues, her sayings oracles, her deeds patterns.[13]

And he continues, sad at heart, that man is so easily lured by the senses and so easily caught up with the beauty of an image.

Southwell's message was for Catholics. He appreciated how hard it was for them to hold out against the strong adverse current of religious conformity. With understanding he wrote these words:

---

[12] R.S. to C.A. (December 28, 1588), F.G. 651.

[13] Ibid.

> It seems no fault to do that all have done:
> The number of offenders hides the sin:
> Coach drawn by many horses doth easily run,
> Soon followeth one where multitudes begin.[14]

From Sussex and East Anglia, Southwell probably passed to the southern midlands. He is so careful to conceal his route—Campion's had been traced and many had suffered in consequence—that there is not a hint of his whereabouts at any time in his letters. But it is probable that he worked on the pattern of houses established by Garnet in this area. He was away still at Christmas, and it is probable that to the winter of 1588 belongs the best known of his poems, "The Burning Babe," about which Ben Jonson declared that he would have destroyed many of his own poems to have written it. Its beauty is enhanced by the spiritual ecstasy that thrills in its lines and is felt so strongly by the reader.

> As I in hoary winter's night
>   Stood shivering in the snow,
> Surpris'd I was with sudden heat,
>   Which made my heart to glow:
>
> And lifting up a fearful eye,
>   To view what fire was near,
> A pretty babe all burning bright
>   Did in the air appear;
>
> Who scorched with excessive heat,
>   Such floods of tears did shed,
> As though his floods should quench his
>   flames,
>   Which with his tears were fed:
>
> Alas (quoth he) but newly born,
>   In fiery heats I fry,
> Yet none approach to warm their
>   hearts,
>   Or feel my fire but I;

---

[14] *Poems.*

> My faultless breast the furnace is,
>> The fuel wounding thorns:
> Love is the fire, and sighs the smoke,
>> The ashes, shame and scorns;
>
> The fuel justice layeth on,
>> And mercy blows the coals,
> The metal in this furnace wrought,
>> Are men's defiled souls:
>
> For which, as now on fire I am
>> To work them for their good,
> So will I melt into a bath,
>> To wash them with my blood.
>
> With this he vanished out of sight,
>> And swiftly shrunk away,
> And straight I called unto mind,
>> That it was Christmas day. (151)

As Southwell felt the fire within him spread, the vision of the Babe vanished. There are probably others among his Christmas poems that belong to this winter. The same theme of the Babe in freezing snow is found again in "New Prince, New Pompe," which, as is true of almost all his poems, cannot be accurately dated.

> Behold a stilly tender Babe
>> In freezing winter night,
> In homely manger trembling lies.
>> Alas, a piteous sight! (16)

"A Vale of Tears," a poem of high lyrical quality, might well also belong to this time. Its rhythm and music combine in a harmony rather more austere but no less rich than in Gray's famous "Elegy," anticipating its romanticism by almost two hundred years. In places it sounds incredibly modern, not unlike a poem of Wordsworth.

The poem expresses the mysteriousness of nature veiling a spiritual reality. Southwell was now thirty, his poetic perception had been sharpened by the daily hazards of his proscribed life. Inspired perhaps by the Derbyshire glades, the nineteen stanzas are a hymn vibrating with awed wonder at the "dreadful shades" in the valley which is thick with "mourning pines" shrouding it from the sun. Through the valleys rush snowy floods with waters that "wrestle with encountering stones" that break their streams and turn them into foam beneath a sky of "hollow clouds full fraught with thundering groans."

The whole of nature now seems to mirror his deep recurrent melancholy:

> All pangs and heavy passions here may find
> A thousand motives suitly to their griefs,
> To feed the sorrows of their troubled mind
> And chase away same pleasure's vain reliefs.

The daytime also matched his musings in a place where "Earth lies forlorn, the cloudy sky doth lower, / The wind here weeps, here sighs, here cries aloud."

But all was not despair. Above the sad valley, through the gaping cliff and beyond some withered trees ashamed of their decay, he saw a mossy plain where "hope doth spring, and there again doth quail" (41).

Always Southwell's poems reflect his contrasting moods. Here the tone is dark as in places of his spiritual notes where he urges himself to "fight manfully and keep up thy spirit . . . for God is trying thee, his own gaze is upon thee." This is repeated in "Seek Flowers of Heaven" in a simple stanza echoing St. Paul's complaint about being kept in his mortal body. He exhorts himself there to

> [s]oar up, my soul, unto thy rest,
> Cast off this loathsome load,
> Long is the date of thy exile,
> Too long thy strait abode. (16)

SIX

A HUMBLE SUPPLICATION

efore they had set out from Rome, Aquaviva had instructed Garnet and Southwell to meet, if possible, twice a year for three days of prayer and spiritual renewal. In the first two years after landing, Garnet had visited Southwell in London, usually in the spring and autumn. But on October 29 in the year of the Armada, as clouds shrouded the night sky, two young Jesuits from Rome had stepped ashore on the sands close to Gromer. They were John Gerard, an aristocrat from Bryn in Lancashire, who could boast that his forebears had been knights for sixteen generations, and Edward Oldcorne, the son of a tradesman of York.

Now that they had arrived, Garnet had to find a refuge in the country where all four of them, sometimes with other priests, could meet in greater safety than was possible in London. Riding with Gerard to what was perhaps their first meeting, Southwell was instructed in all the finer points of falconry, in which Gerard had been proficient from his youth. It was a subject that both found useful when riding in the company of gentlemen who, as Gerard put it, "had practically no other conversation apart perhaps from obscene subjects and rant against the saints and the Catholic faith."[1] Moreover, talk about falcons provided a convenient mask for the priests' identities.

Although a countryman like Gerard, Southwell had spent the greater part of his boyhood days abroad and found it difficult to learn the lessons that Gerard was anxious to teach him: the terms were difficult and it was easy to trip up in their correct use. "Frequently," wrote Gerard, "when Robert was travelling with me, he would ask me to explain the correct terms and would worry when he could not remember them all and use them as the need arose." But Southwell worked hard on them and occasionally in his writings, perhaps after revision from Gerard, would venture on a protracted metaphor drawn from falconry.[2]

Throughout the days the priests were together, Garnet advised, encouraged, and sustained the spirit of the men working under his direction. New hopes took shape, fresh plans were formed, adjustments made in the distribution of priests as each year more Jesuits joined him or as seminary priests put themselves at his disposition.

Southwell wrote rapturously to Aquaviva of these meetings. "Thanks to your prayers, we can hope that springtime will soon be at hand, with the flowers appearing and the vineyards spreading their fragrance. We strive for this with all our strength in this rocky and desert land, hearing each other's confessions every six months and renewing our vows."[3]

On one occasion when all the Jesuits and some seminary priests were together at Baddesley Clinton in Warickshire, the house was raided. It was early morn-

---

[1] John Gerard, *The Autobiography of an Elizabethan,* trans. and ed. Philip Caraman, S.J. (Longmans, 1951).

[2] Ibid.

[3] R.S. to C.A. (December 28, 1588), F.G. 651.

ing; Southwell was offering Mass before taking to the
road, the maidservants were occupied preparing breakfast, the stablemen were saddling the horses when the
house was surrounded by pursuivants. Only a well-con-
structed hiding place in the disused sewer saved the
lives of the priests. Hidden there they prayed together
until the search was called off.

Although Southwell was aware that the net was
closing in on him, yet he was able now to face with
composure, and even with a smile, the prospect of an
early violent death that would inevitably follow his
capture. "A certain nobleman," Garnet told Aquaviva,
"once said to me that when he was going for a walk
with Father Robert by London Bridge, he saw his face
light up with an extraordinary gaiety when he looked
up at the martyrs' heads placed there and said, 'My
Lord, if God grants it, you will see one day my head on
one of those pikes.'"[4]

Still his finest prose was to come, inspired by
blazing indignation at the slander of his fellow priests
and former students, whom he had taught in Rome and
who were now sharing the dangers of his present life.
Although the Armada had been scattered, the threat
from Spain remained. There was still a Spanish army in
the Netherlands and nearer still a Spanish-French force
in Normandy assembled to expel Henry IV from
France. The Queen was quick to note that Spain had
bases across the Channel from which it would be easy
to launch an invasion. As on the eve of the Armada,
new measures were contemplated for the repression of
Catholics. Because Parliament was not sitting, the
Queen in Council issued a Proclamation dated October
18, 1591. It bore the title "A declaration of great trou-
bles pretended against the realm by a number of semi-

---

[4] H.G. to C.A. (May 1, 1595), F.G. 651.

nary priests and Jesuits, sent and very secretly dispersed in the same, to work great treasons under a false pretence of religion, with a provision very necessary for the remedy thereof."

The new measures against Catholics added little to the laws already in force against them; what was new was the virulence of the language of the proclamation. The seminary priests were branded a multitude of dissolute young men, who partly for lack of a living, partly for crimes committed in England, had become fugitives, rebels, and traitors. They were denounced as "very base by birth" and "venomous vipers" or "unnatural subjects of our kingdom."

This was propaganda that was likely to do more permanent damage to the Catholic community than the new measures of repression contained in the proclamation.

The replies came quickly. Robert Persons, who had taken his farewell of Southwell at the Milvian Bridge five years earlier, replied section by section in language that yielded little in scurrility to the Council. Three other books written abroad followed in the same year. But their virulence of language served only to add to the persecution of Catholics at home. Southwell, aware of this, wrote in dignified phrases direct to the Queen, whom in total sincerity he addressed as "Most mighty and most merciful, most feared and best beloved Princess."

In his discernment of the Council's mind, Southwell interpreted the proclamation differently from his coreligionists abroad. He saw in it a note of panic: the persecution had failed in its aim; the sheer bloodshed had achieved the reverse end from what had been intended; perhaps he read an indication of alarm at his own and Garnet's success in the phrase referring to the priests as "very secretly dispersed" in the kingdom.

Although *An Humble Supplication,* Southwell's
reply, is written in the form of a letter to the Queen, it
is unlikely that he expected it to reach her. Probably he
intended it to be printed at Garnet's press, but at the
time of his arrest on June 25, 1592, it was still circulating only in handwritten copies. William Weston saw a
copy that reached him in prison at Wisbech, and wrote
that he had read it "immediately after it was completed
in manuscript and circulated among a few friends."[5]
Another copy came into the hands of Southwell's cap-
tor and tormentor, Richard Topcliffe. Topcliffe showed
it to Francis Bacon, Southwell's cousin, who admired
the way Southwell in his heated defense of his fellow
priests had written without conceits.[6] Answering the
charge of the "baseness" of the priests' birth, Southwell
wrote that he did "not mean to dwell long on it, for the
thing neither importeth any offence to God nor crime
against your Majesty, nor greatly abaseth them, whom
excellent virtues—the only true measures of worthi-
ness—have ennobled." Cardinal Allen, who had been
maligned by name, Southwell championed as a man of
"as good and ancient house" as any of the Councilors.[7]
Then "as for other priests, how many of them are
knights' sons and squires' sons, and otherwise allied to
worshipful and noble houses and heirs of fair reve-
nues." Altogether "in the small number of Catholic
priests of our nation (which reacheth not to a tenth of
the Protestant ministry) there are very near as many,

---

[5] W.W., 99.

[6] From Gray's Inn on May 5, 1894, Francis Bacon wrote to
his brother Anthony: "I send you the Supplication which Mr
Topcliffe lent me. It is curiously written and worth the writing out,
though the argument be bad" (James Spedding, *Letters and Life of
Francis Bacon* [London, 1861], 2:308).

[7] *Humble Supplication,* 5.

yea happily more, gentlemen than in all the other cler-
gy of the whole realm" (7).

It was to save priests from further almost intoler-
able pain that Southwell exposed in terrible detail the
loathsome tortures to which they were subjected.
"Some priests," he writes,

> are hanged by the hands eight or nine or twelve hours
> together till not only their wits but even their senses fail
> them, and when the soul, weary of so painful an har-
> bour, is ready to depart, they apply cruel comforts and
> revive us only to martyr us with more deaths. . . . Some,
> besides their tortures have been forced to lie continually
> booted and clothed many weeks together, pined in their
> diet, consumed with vermin, and almost stifled with
> stench. Some have been watched and kept from sleep
> till they were past the use of reason, and then examined
> upon the advantage, when they could scarcely give ac-
> count of their own names. . . . Some with instruments
> have been rolled up like a ball and so crushed that the
> blood sprouted out at divers parts of their bodies. (34)

Then omitting other cruelties, he refers to the contin-
ual purgatory of priests suffering in the notorious
Bridewell Prison.

Although Southwell intended the *Humble Supplication* to be printed, Garnet judged it prudent to
disallow its circulation beyond some handwritten
copies. Several reasons brought him to that decision.
He hoped that the storm created by the proclamation
would pass sooner if Catholics endured abuse passively.
He had seen no good come from the vituperative
pamphleteering that had preceded the Spanish
Armada. It was the behavior rather than the writings of
Catholics that would prove false the allegations against
them, a view that was vindicated within a month of the
proclamation, when three priests—Edmund Jennings,
Eustace White, and Polydore Plasden—were
condemned as traitors on the sole charge of their

ordination abroad. The savagery of their execution
stirred the crowds to sympathy and caused Southwell to
insert in the *Supplication* the sentence of the Lord
Chief Justice, who when condemning them stated that
he was pronouncing sentence only upon the statute of
their coming into England after being ordained priests
abroad.

Southwell's approach to the crisis was little appreciated by the leading Catholic exiles. The polemics
produced by English priests on the Continent could
only have troubled Garnet, who feared they would lead
to retaliation at home. Although this apprehension did
not include Southwell's *Supplication,* there was danger
of another kind in its appearance. The very form in
which it was written and its fulsome praise of the
Queen might lead to further misunderstandings between Catholics at home and abroad. Moreover, Garnet knew that its publication would be tantamount to
the sacrifice of Southwell's life. The search for him,
which was already unrelenting, would be intensified,
and Garnet was in no mood to hand over his dearest
friend to Richard Topcliffe by permitting the diffusion
of the book. No priest, not at least since the time of
Campion, had championed the Catholic cause with
such scalding conviction and eloquence. Only Garnet
was in a position to appreciate all that his companion
had done for English Catholics. The publication of the
Supplication was too high a price to pay for the passing
satisfaction of the Catholic community.

The hunt for priests had so intensified that Garnet, always short of help, was now convinced that it
would be wise to hold back on the Continent newly
ordained men destined for England. "It is not worth
the risk of sending them," he advised, "unless they are
anxious to rush headlong into peril and dire poverty
. . . conditions are so unfavourable. If God does not

intervene things will reach the verge of ruin. There is no place that is safe."[8] He was not writing in a mood of dejection, but with an objective assessment of the situation, which was even worse than Garnet described it a few months before the proclamation. "Many Catholics," he had then written,

> change their dwelling places [in order to receive the sacraments] and go, as it were into voluntary exile, and live unknown and obscurely in remote parts of the country. If there were some one place where they might be permitted to live in peace, they would consider themselves treated fairly enough. But the faithful are not left to themselves anywhere. It is impossible save at the greatest risk to baptise infants, celebrate marriages, give the sacraments or to offer the sacrifice according to the Catholic rite. Expectant mothers have to travel to far-away places for the birth of their infants in order not to be asked about the christening of their offspring.[9]

Garnet's own reply to the proclamation was very personal. From the start of his missionary work, he had encouraged Catholics to enroll themselves in a pious sodality known as the Confraternity of the Rosary. At no time did he doubt that the fight for the old religion was to be won mainly by spiritual weapons. From his own experience he set great store by the merits and prayers of the martyred priests, and it was this that made him their first and most detailed historian. He treasured also the prayers of his Roman friends. Whenever he wrote to Aquaviva, he included a petition for his prayers and the prayers of his Roman friends. In Rome he had witnessed a growing devotion to the rosary. When Pius V had called for a crusade against the Turks, he urged all Catholics to support it with the regular recital of the rosary. Devout persons in all

---

[8] H.G. to C.A. (February 11, 1592), F.G. 651.

[9] H.G. to C.A. (May 25, 1590), F.G. 651.

countries attributed the victory of Lepanto to the widespread use of the rosary in the churches of Rome and Italy. Garnet himself had witnessed the inauguration of the Feast of the Rosary by Gregory XIII in 1573. Before leaving for England, he had received from the Dominican General special faculties, reserved normally to the friars of that order, to admit English Catholics into the confraternity. A crusader at heart, he believed that this prayer would be effective against heresy in England as it had been against the Albigenses in the time of St. Dominic.

While Southwell was engaged on the *Supplication,* Garnet wrote his first published English work, *The Societie of the Rosary.* The title page explains his intention. There the antiphon of the office of our Lady is printed: "Gaude Virgo Maria, cunctas hereses sola interemisti in universo mundo" (Rejoice, Virgin Mary, since thou alone hast crushed all heresies throughout the world).

In October 1591 Garnet wrote urgently to Aquaviva, reminding him that he had already asked him for a renewal of his special privileges regarding the confraternity, for he feared that they had lapsed with the death of the Dominican General, Sixtus Fabri, in 1589. Now he added a request for the new Master General to grant a dispensation from the rule that the names of members should be inscribed in a book. It was one thing to allow Catholics to risk arrest by keeping rosary beads secretly in their homes, another to draw up lists of members that might fall into the hands of the priest hunters and quickly bring ruin on their homes. To spread the devotion more rapidly, Garnet was anxious that more English priests should be given the faculties that he himself had been granted.

The book was widely diffused. When the stock of the first edition was seized in a raid on Garnet's press, a second edition was out within a year. An engraving of the Virgin with her infant Son appeared on the new title page. This was Garnet's hope against heresy. He was "fully persuaded" that Catholics should enlist on their side the power of our Lady's intercession and "obtain from her a new rainbow, which being a sign of God, cannot signify falsely, but must certainly foretell our comfort and relief."[10]

---

[10] Preface to *The Societie of the Rosary,* (1592); See H.G., 143-45.

SEVEN

A VERY SPECIAL KIND
OF COURAGE

In March 1590 Southwell had written, "My companion and I [this was the way he usually referred to Garnet in his letters to Aquaviva] after avoiding Scylla proceeded to steer into Charybdis, but by a special mercy of God we circumvented both and are now riding safely at anchor."[1]

He does not specify the particular danger. His relief at the escape was short-lived. The arch-pursuivant, Richard Topcliffe, had made him perhaps the most sought-after priest in England.

Topcliffe's position is difficult to define. Although the only official position he held was that of Queen's pursuivant, he possessed almost despotic power. Responsible only to his sovereign, he had his own private gang of thugs who shared with him the spoils of his conquests. He organized raids and directed them in person; he was both grand inquisitor and rack master, possessing a license to torture privately on his own premises. At the trial of priests, he was assistant prosecutor; at the scaffold, assistant director of executions. He boasted that he had the ear of the Queen. Garnet spoke of him as *homo sordidissimus.* "This most sordid

---

[1] R.S. to C.A. (March 8, 1590), C.R.S., 5:330.

of men," he wrote "need not fear the power or influence of any Councillor or Minister."[2]

Topcliffe, moreover, had devised a new form of torture, more efficient, slow, silent, and merciless than the old-fashioned rack: his helpless victim, his feet off the ground, was hung from a rod passed through rings pinned against a wall. In this way the body did the work of pulleys and weights. The method of torture was so simple that he was able at trivial expense to equip his torture room in an annex to the prison off Fleet Street. Hitherto torture had been used only in the Tower. Its use anywhere was contrary to common law, but was justified by Tudor lawyers on the ground that the sovereign, by the exercise of personal prerogative, could by this means force political prisoners to reveal secrets injurious to the state. Something of this pretence had been maintained in the devices practiced on Edmund Campion, Ralph Sherwin, and Arthur Bryant. But after the act of 1585 making it treason for a subject of the Queen to receive Orders abroad and return to England afterwards, it was no longer necessary to seek to involve priests in a plot against the state before proceeding to their trial. Nevertheless, warrants were issued to Topcliffe for indiscriminate torture as a means of extorting from priests information that would lead to the capture of their brethren.

Topcliffe's rise to favor brought with it a more systematic search for priests. His own mad zeal spurred on local magistrates, particularly in the home counties, to frenzied activity. He was ubiquitous in the south; occasionally he was seen in his native Yorkshire. Everywhere he threatened to delate any justices of the peace who were less active than himself, accusing them of being sympathetic to Catholics.

---

[2] H.G. to C.A. (July 16, 1592), F.G. 651.

There were many reasons why Southwell should have become Topcliffe's most sought-after prize. Not only was he the principal "receiver" of priests, but he was the most available and esteemed counselor in their personal difficulties. It was to his authority, and to Garnet's, that they appealed in times of crisis. In addition to posting priests to country stations, Southwell supervised the dispatch of an ever growing number of students to the seminaries abroad. He had gifts that made him outstanding in his pastoral work. "So wise, good, gentle and loveable," as Garnet wrote of him, his influence among families of importance and on the fringe of the court was increasing every year.[3] Some of his writings were now circulating fairly widely. It was not surprising that he was known as the "chief dealer of Papists in England," a name by which Topcliffe described him about this time.

Without Southwell knowing it, a description of his physical appearance had come into the hands of the Council. It had been provided by a priest, John Cecil, who had been with him in Rome. After being arrested in the spring of 1591, Cecil had stated that Southwell was a beardless, auburn-haired young man of medium height and youthful appearance. It was not much to go on, but it was to prove sufficient for Topcliffe to identify his prey.[4]

In preparation for Southwell's capture, his pursuer launched a campaign of denigration. It dealt mainly with his alleged unfair treatment of priests. In particular, he was accused of turning away from his door Thomas Pormont, a future martyr. The lie, however, was nailed by another priest, Thomas Standish, who testified that Southwell, on the contrary,

---

[3] Ibid.

[4] Devlin.

> gave him [Pormont] a wonderful welcome on his arrival
> in England. He fed him and clothed him and brought
> him with honor into his own house, which is a mark of
> singular esteem in times of persecution. He also found
> him twenty crowns, introduced him to friends of very
> high rank and established him in as safe a shelter as
> possible.[5]

Garnet adds that Pormont until the time of his arrest "never ceased to follow Robert's advice in all things."

As the search for Southwell and other priests became more systematic, Garnet took the unusual step of not calling a meeting in the early part of 1592. "There is nowhere left to hide," he wrote to Aquaviva in February of that year. Though never fatalistic, he seems to have had foreknowledge of imminent disaster. Throughout the spring and early summer, he appears to have been expecting news of Southwell's arrest. When finally it came, he showed no surprise. "This was by no means a sudden and unforeseen misfortune. For a long time now it had been planned by our enemies," he wrote soon after Southwell's arrest.

The trap had been set by a young woman, Anne, the daughter of Robert Bellamy of Uxenden Hall at Harrow. When a prisoner for the faith in the Gatehouse near Westminster Abbey, she was found pregnant after three months. Her father's letter to the Council leaves little doubt that it was Topcliffe who had raped her. In her misery she was told that she could save her family from persecution if she could entice Southwell to Uxenden and betray him there to Topcliffe. Garnet, possibly with a premonition that something was afoot, sent Southwell word to ride out

---

[5] H.G. to C.A. (July 16, 1592), F.G. 651. The account of R.S.'s arrest in the following pages is taken from this letter, and from a second letter written to C.A. ten days later, July 26, 1592 (Westminster Archives, 4, 305).

to Warickshire. "He had actually planned the journey," he wrote, "when he received an invitation to the honoured household of the Bellamys, which had long lacked a consoler, and so he arranged to spend his first night there."

The Bellamy household had been one of the oldest and safest of Jesuit resorts in England. Persons had met the family during his short visit twelve years earlier. Campion had been there and it was the first household to give Weston shelter. Both Garnet and Southwell had visited it a number of times. While Garnet suspected treachery from within, he was careful not to state this until it was established.

Southwell arrived at Uxenden on the morning of June 24. At once, in Garnet's phrase, he had "given comfort in his usual manner to almost all there present—to the family, friends and retainers." The word "almost" excluded Anne, for the comforting consisted in confession, Mass, and Communion. It was Southwell's last Mass. Instead of continuing his journey the same day, he yielded to the pressing invitation of his hostess to remain until the following morning.

That night Topcliffe surrounded the house. Never before had he gone out of London in such strength, "a vast swarm," says Garnet, composed of jailbirds and meaner courtiers wearing the Queen's escutcheon, armed to the teeth. On the road he gathered fresh forces when he was joined by a magistrate of Middlesex. He could take no chances. After all his boasting that he would capture Southwell, his failure to do so would have brought his hideous career to a crisis. Garnet suspected this.

After his forces had been disposed round the house, Topcliffe began his assault. Immediately the alarm was raised. Mrs. Bellamy rushed Southwell into the hiding place. As Topcliffe broke into the house, he had all the men servants bound hand and foot. The rest of the household was heavily guarded. Topcliffe, after upbraiding Mrs. Bellamy in disgusting language, produced a piece of paper from his pocket and read a description of the hiding place. He then ordered her to "hand over this Cotton," a name which Southwell was in the habit of using, "or I shall pull this foul nest about your ears, beam by beam."

"I know no man of that name," she protested. Then she realized that only one of the family could have provided Topcliffe with such a correct description of the hiding place. She still refused, however; but somehow, possibly by a prearranged sign, she was able to communicate with Southwell, leaving the choice of action to him. Southwell, in Garnet's words, judged that the game was up and presented himself before Topcliffe there and then.

As Southwell entered the hall, Topcliffe paused in his flow of abuse. It is unlikely that he had seen Southwell before. But the description he had been given tallied.

> The slim straight build, the auburn hair, the famous eyes with their arched brows, the finely cut lips set in a slight smile that might be called mockery if it were not so mild and courteous; and not the description only, but a certain air of something undefinable, something absolute, proclaimed that this was the man.[6]

As they faced each other, Topcliffe quivered with frenzy. He demanded who he was. "A gentleman," was Southwell's answer. Then Topcliffe swore, "No, a priest, a traitor, a Jesuit." Calmly Southwell asked him to prove each assertion; for if he admitted his identity, he would bring appalling penalties on his hostess. In his

---

[6] This is Christopher Devlin's description based on a probable likeness. See Devlin, 281 and note.

uncontrollable wrath, Topcliffe momentarily forgot the importance of seizing his prey alive. He ran at Southwell with his sword. Southwell stood his ground as Topcliffe's men rushed forward and held their master back. Impassively Southwell looked Topcliffe in the eye, beholding the torturer of his former students. This was more than the man could bear. He accused Southwell of denying his priesthood through fear. He called him "the filthiest traitor in the kingdom." With irony and masterly choice of words, Southwell replied, "No, it is neither priest nor traitor you are seeking but only blood. And if mine will satisfy you, then you shall have it as freely as my mother gave it to me. And if it will not satisfy, I do not doubt but you shall find many more as willing as myself." He concluded with a priestly warning: "Only I would advise you to remember that there is a God, and that He is just in his judgements, and therefore blood will have blood, but I rather wish your conversion."

"We came to arrest you," interrupted Topcliffe, "not to listen to your prattling."

Topcliffe then dispatched a messenger to Greenwich with news for the Queen of his latest success; she "heard it, I am told," says Garnet, who had it straight from the court, "with unwonted merriment."

The house was ransacked and the chapel furnishings thrown into a cart along with Southwell himself and taken to Topcliffe's house in Westminster. "With the first light of morning," writes Garnet,

> he was taken to London and though they had only the less frequented streets to traverse, yet immediately the report of his capture spread through the city, and more swiftly than one can believe, it was bruited abroad through the whole kingdom. It is not possible to describe the sorrow of Catholics (and not only of Catholics). It was as if each one had lost a dear friend.

Understandably, Garnet first wrote to Aquaviva, then later to Persons, for Southwell had formed closer ties with him than with Persons. But he waited two weeks before writing, in order to make certain of the facts. Even then he was careful to distinguish between what he had heard himself and what he had learned from others. He was anxious not to spread any false or exaggerated stories. "I thought it good," he writes, "to advise you of the whole truth as far as I could in any way learn it."

In these two letters, written under the stress of emotion, Garnet uncovers his soul as in no other place. For his first two years in England, Southwell had been his only Jesuit assistant. Although he occasionally refers to him as "Robert," he more usually calls him his "companion." Southwell had also been his friend, confidant, and confessor. There had been no anxiety, decision, or hope that he had not shared with him since they landed together on the coast to the east of Folkestone.

Although they did not meet again in the next two and a half years, Garnet took every opportunity that presented itself to catch a glimpse of his companion. When Southwell was transferred from one prison to another or taken from the Tower for trial at Westminster Hall, Garnet was there among the crowd and at once reported to Aquaviva on his carriage, dignity, and the expression of his countenance.

Southwell more than Garnet was a public figure moving at ease among nobles, courtiers, poets, while Garnet quietly organized the "churches" in the shires. After Southwell's arrest it is possible to discern a change in Garnet. Something of his self-confidence has gone. He is more anxious, hesitating, and easily alarmed. Neither Gerard or any other priest could replace his "companion."

"At length and at last," he opened his letter to Aquaviva, "it has happened. . . . After a peaceful and prosperous voyage lasting six years, we have encountered fierce and tempestuous seas. . . . Our very gentle dear companion has been captured by pirates, and now in a broken and battered vessel we are sailing without a helmsman."

Southwell was the helmsman, Garnet the captain. Garnet's first reaction to the news of his companion's capture must have been relief that he had not allowed the publication of the *Humble Supplication,* for Southwell would now have the comfort of standing trial and facing torture and imprisonment with the issue of his priesthood unclouded by politics. Garnet felt that he in God's design had been "passed over": Southwell had been chosen before him "because God did not judge me fit for such a contest."

Southwell had long prepared himself for this moment. "He is an undutiful child," he had once written,

> that is ashamed who is his father, and a most malapert servant that refuseth to wear his master's livery; but the most ungrateful creature of all is he that doth not willingly accept the livery of his God and maker. If we be Christians, affliction is our coat and the cross our cognizance.[7]

His conscience was clear. He had been long repentant of what he considered his sins and failures, and this was to strengthen him in the years still ahead.

> If David night by night did bath his bed,
> Esteeming longest days too short to moan
> . . . .

---

[7] *Epistle of Comfort,* 30.

> Then I to days and weeks, to months and
>   years
> Do owe the hourly rent of stintless tears.[8]

Although at first the Queen was delighted at the capture of Southwell, whose pen she admired and feared at the same time, Southwell before long was to become an embarrassment to her.

No arrest of a priest had caused such sadness to Catholics since Campion's. But Garnet was confident that his companion's example in suffering would be an immeasurable force for good. He feared, however, for him now at Topcliffe's mercy. He knew that in Topcliffe's house unknown tortures awaited him, for here several priests had already endured unspeakable suffering. As these thoughts came into his mind, he put them down on paper. Southwell, he told Aquaviva, "is so well prepared that, stricken as we are, we feel that God by his suffering will increase his glory and the good of the Church. . . . But a very special kind of courage is needed to endure these tortures. . . . Our hope is in the mystical body of Christ and in the mutual compassion of its members."

The license allowed by the Queen to Topcliffe can be explained only by the undertaking given by him that he would force all priests to confess that they were traitors. The facts, however, did not fit his claim. No matter how he dealt with them, his victims could only be brought to admit their priesthood. It was only gradually that Garnet learned the extent of his companion's sufferings.

Within ten days of Southwell's arrest, Garnet gathered some shocking details from friends connected with the court and from prisoners at the Gatehouse.

---

[8] *Poems,* 90.

After twenty-four hours during which Topcliffe hung
Southwell from the rods attached to the wall, he was
compelled to confess defeat. No word that could be
construed as treachery could be extracted from him. In
a further message to the Queen, Topcliffe admitted his
failure. The Queen branded Topcliffe a fool and sent
him a return message to say that she and her
councilors would take over Southwell's examination.

Among the men chosen by the Queen to continue
the questioning was the clerk of the Privy Council, Sir
William Wade, who on several occasions had entangled
priests in their statements. He was given an assistant
who is unnamed. "Nevertheless," says Garnet, "the
prisoner remained obdurate." On Tuesday night or on
early Wednesday morning, June 28, Wade had Southwell removed from Topcliffe's house to the Gatehouse
at Westminster. It was feared, perhaps, that Southwell
might die in Topcliffe's hands. Now he was examined
more systematically, hung up more frequently, and
deliberately deprived of sleep.

Garnet could get only fragmentary details of what
passed within the walls of Southwell's new prison. He
discovered the cell in which he was confined and noted
that the windows had been shuttered from the outside
and that the only light entered through a pane of glass
set in the ceiling.

But Garnet learned one startling piece of news.
After Wade had failed to extract from Southwell a
statement of guilt, Robert Cecil had taken part in the
examination. Cecil had been prepared by Wade for a
display of obstinacy. But from the drawn, tortured
figure hanging from the wall in front of him, he could
elicit only reasoned replies. When questions touched
the lives and whereabouts of his Catholic hosts,
Southwell was silent. It was a scene Cecil was never to
forget. Some years later, when he was riding out of

London with a friend, he recalled the sight. "They boast about the heroes of antiquity," he said, "but we have a new torture that is not possible for a man to endure. And yet I have seen Robert Southwell hanging by it, still as a tree trunk, and none able to drag a word from his mouth." "Semper pertinax" was the summary of Garnet's tribute to his companion. Never had he doubted that he would remain steadfast.

Garnet knew that Southwell was at peace deep in his soul. In the final stanzas of his last poem, which he left unfinished at the time of his arrest, Southwell had prepared himself in spirit for these very trials. With sorrow for all he had done amiss, he had prayed in these words:

> Let true remorse my due revenge abate:
> Let tears appease when trespass doth incense:
> Let pity temper thy deserved hate.
> Let grace forgive, let love forget my fall:
> With fear I crave, with hope I humbly call.
>
> Redeem my lapse with ransom of thy love,
> Traverse th' indictment, rigor's doom suspend:
> Let frailty favour, sorrow succour move:
> Be thou thyself, though changing I offend,
> Tender my suite, cleanse this defiled den,
> Cancel my debts, sweet Jesu, say Amen.[9]

Garnet's epistolary style changes with Southwell's arrest. He is more direct, uninhibited, and hurried. In describing his friend's sufferings, he reveals himself as never before. There existed in England no more intimate friendship between two priests than between him and Southwell. They had many bonds of affection with shared trials to secure them. Often they had spoken together about Topcliffe. Both had written to Aquaviva about his iniquities. Both knew his story:

---

[9] *Poems,* 99f.

How at the age of sixty, with his fortune in ruins, he had striven to reestablish himself at the price of priests' lives. "Entering now the course of honour that you now see him following," wrote Garnet with sarcasm, "he boasts that he gets more pleasure from hunting down priests than he ever got from chasing wild animals or setting snares for birds."

Garnet now felt unspeakably lonely. Both by temperament and outlook he was separated from other English Jesuits. He appreciated the loyalty of all his priests, and on their side they revered him as their superior; but none could take the place of his companion. In his search for the kind of support Southwell had given him, he grew closer to Aquaviva with every letter he wrote to Rome.

At the same time he thanked God for the support Southwell had given him for more years than he had expected. He felt assured that their fates had been ordered by Providence. "While I cannot help myself in my sadness and anxiety . . . deprived as I now am of my companion my dearest father and my helper, I await his greatest achievements yet." Then he returns to two reflections. "Southwell was so well prepared," he assures Aquaviva,

> that stricken as we are we feel that God through his sufferings will enhance his glory, strengthen his church and confound his enemies. . . . A very special kind of courage is required to endure these tortures. . . . What seems insufferable for one person, when it is shared by all the members [of the mystical body] becomes sweet indeed, not by any means because it is less severe, but by reason of the love that binds us all together. This truly is to bear one another's burdens: it is the mutual compassion of members whereby the weakness of one is supported by the strength of another.

Garnet wrote this both to comfort himself in Southwell's sufferings and to allay his own fears. His dread of physical torture was intense. Frequently he had doubts whether he would be able to endure what others had borne. He made no secret of this, as he had no doubts of Southwell's powers of endurance. "I have drawn great consolation from my companion's state, for never has he been known to disappoint the expectations friends have held of him." The daily companionship was now replaced by a mystical fellowship. In his search for grounds of comfort, he becomes one of the first Englishmen to develop at some length St. Paul's doctrine of the mystical body of Christ.

Towards the end of the letter, Garnet pulls down his last reserves. He felt that his own days of freedom were now few; that Providence was indicating that as he and Southwell had begun their mission together, so they would end it together. He wrote dramatically: He might be arrested before he came to sign the letter, or perhaps before it reached Rome. His quarters might be exposed as carrion for the crows on London Bridge. At best he expected that this would be the last letter he would write and forewarned Aquaviva that he might show frailty if he were subjected to the same treatment as Southwell. The search for him had been almost as persistent and as widespread as the search for Southwell. Public feeling had been stirred up against him. He calls on Aquaviva not to relax his prayers.

> Since we are never safe, never out of danger, it is right that your concern for us should never cease; and now more than ever before because since the coming of the Spanish fleet into these waters, far more than any other priest in the country I am suspect of stirring sedition and rallying Catholics to support the King of Spain. For me and for none other the tortures are already prescribed.

Although Garnet now expressed his emotions freely, he never made a statement of fact without careful inquiry. He knew that Southwell was being racked behind the shuttered window in order to reveal his own whereabouts. It required very little insight to discern the policy of the government. Burleigh had well in hand his plans to detach the Catholic body in England from the Holy See, then split it brutally asunder. If Southwell or Garnet could be induced to confess criminal plottings, then Burleigh had won the day. In his letter to the Queen after Southwell's capture, Topcliffe had boasted that he had "never taken so weighty a man" and was confident that he could make him reveal "anything in his heart [by making him] to stand against the wall, his feet standing upon the ground and his hands stuck as high as he can reach against the wall like a trick at Trenchmore.[10] This will enforce him to tell all, and the truth proved by the sequel." It would have been unnatural of Garnet not to admit his fears when he got details of Southwell's treatment.

His reflections jostle each other in this letter.

> I distrust myself as well I may, and my misery makes me pause. Yet when I consider the goodness of God, the strength my calling gives me, the common ties that bind me to so many saintly men and to so many valiant servants of Christ, I begin already to envy my companion and grieve that while he has been taken to receive a crown of immeasurable glory, I have been kept for battles yet unknown. It is the way God acts in the spiritual combat.

He goes on to contrast Southwell's role as a front-line fighter with his own part that requires an organizer in the rear. "The soldier that fights at a distance remains remote from the scene of victory, which God decrees

---

[10] Trenchmore, a boisterous dance of the period. Topcliffe expected Southwell to dance in that fashion on the rack under torture.

should now hang in the balance. When the fight has been brought close to the enemy, God assures the triumph of all he chooses for this part." Then drawing comfort from the suffering of all his priest friends, he adds, "When the harvest of all their merits shall be gathered in for the year, then I shall not lack strength to undertake any great work whatsoever or endure whatsoever may happen to me."

The spontaneous affection Garnet had given Southwell he now poured out on Aquaviva. He was certain that the General on his side was grateful for the confidence he placed in him. Declining Garnet's proposal that he should hand over responsibility for the Jesuit mission in England to another priest, Aquaviva replied by giving him still-greater support and sympathy. Garnet needed it. For several months now there had been rumors of grumbling opposition to the Jesuits.

In closing the letter, Garnet wrote that he was leaving London, uncertain when he would return. It was "too hot" for him in the capital. Possibly through his friends who had given him news of Southwell, he had learned that Topcliffe was now in pursuit of him. To capture both within the month was a coup that would partially make up for his failure to get any incriminating statement from Southwell. Garnet, on the other hand, might yield. But in any case, by lies and cunning he could play off one against the other, as he was later to do when he had both Southwell and Gerard in his hands. Garnet's last act before leaving London was to arrange for a breviary to be sent to Southwell. The countess of Arundel added a volume of St. Bernard's sermons and a consignment of clothes and bedding.

"A Goliath of fortitude" was his last word in praise of his companion.

EIGHT

KEPT CLOSE PRISONER

I t was sometime in July that Southwell was tortured for the last time. Towards the end of that month, he was still in the Gatehouse Prison, helpless and feeble in body, unable to attend to himself, covered with maggots and his own filth. But his spirit was unbroken. He had won his contest. The councilors were defeated.

In the Privy Council Register there is an order dated July 28 requiring the lieutenant of the Tower to "receive Rob. Southwell priest to be kept close prisoner so that no one may be suffered access to him but such anyone as Topcliffe shall appoint as his keeper."[1] There is an addition probably made by Topcliffe himself: "Herein we require you to take order for his close restraining, he being a most lewd and dangerous person."

The transference to the Tower was probably granted at the petition of Robert's father, Richard Southwell. He had asked that

> if his son had committed anything for which by the laws he deserved death, he might suffer death. If not, as he was a gentleman, that her majesty might be pleased to order that he should be treated as such, even though he

---

[1] Privy Council Registers, vol. X, f.504.

were a Jesuit. And that as his father he might be permitted to send him what he needed to sustain life.[2]

This petition was granted. Richard Southwell, who
was bankrupt at the time, would nevertheless have had
friends at court to support his petition. But the only
person actually permitted to visit Southwell in the
Gatehouse was his sister, Mary Bannister, who was
probably one of Garnet's informants. Southwell's heroic
resistance was now well known and the details of his
suffering had caused deep if not widespread anger.

It may well have been that the Queen's attention
had been brought to the fact that her Jesuit prisoner,
who had written the learned *Humble Supplication,*
belonged to a family well known to her and could claim
cousinship with her chief minister; that he himself was
the son of the girl with whom she had been brought up
and with whom she had learned the Latin tongue.

There could also have been political motives for
her clemency. Solitary confinement in the Tower would
cause Southwell to be forgotten. It might also break his
resolve. In any case, after the execution of Polydore
Plasden and his two companions on December 16,
1591, she was reluctant to bring a priest to trial save on
the pretext of plotting or treachery. It was better to let
the clamor caused by Southwell's arrest die down
quietly. On leaving the Gatehouse, he was permitted to
take with him a Bible and the works of St. Bernard
that the countess of Arundel had added to the breviary
that Garnet had sent him.

Garnet needed rest and leisure. He left London
for the countryside after Southwell had been
transferred to the Tower. There some areas could be
found that were comparatively unaffected by heresy, as

---

[2] Pierre Janelle, *Robert Southwell, the Writer* (Sheed and
Ward, 1935), 68 n. 35.

Gerard had discovered on landing in Norfolk. On
August 15 and again on September 5, 1592, he had
written to Aquaviva, but neither of these letters had
reached Rome. He was impatient to receive some word
of comfort from the General. Nervously fatigued, he
took several months to recover his health. Writing a
third time on October 8, he realized how agitated he
had been: "Since every letter I write increases your
Lordship's concern for us," he wrote,

> I try as much as I am able to send you more frequent
> letters. On 4 September I gave you news of my
> companion. What I said then holds still. He is kept in
> the royal prison [the Tower] and is hidden from the
> clamour of his persecutors. He is not allowed to see any
> friends, but apart from this he is now being treated with
> some humanity by the Lieutenant of the Tower.[3]

Garnet repeated once more that he was in need of
Aquaviva's affection and counsel.

During his visit to the country, Garnet saw that
the determination of Catholics was unchanged and that
the system he had built up with Southwell had
withstood this latest shock of persecution. He remained
absent from London all through the autumn. The
plague was raging in the city and the assizes had been
canceled. There had been no further news of Southwell
when he left, so he ended his letter briefly: "I beg your
Lordship to send me an assistant [to replace Southwell]
for I cannot live continually in London except at very

---

[3] H.G. to C.A. (October 8, 1592), F.G. 651. This lieutenant
was Sir Richard Berkeley, who was succeeded in June 1597 by Sir
John Peyton. John Gerard, referring to his own torture in the Tower
and to his escape in October 1597, writes, "A gentleman of position
told me that he had heard Sir Richard Berkeley say . . . that he had
freely resigned his office because he no longer wished to be an
instrument in such torture of innocent men" [namely, Southwell and
himself] (*John Gerard,* 114).

great peril. I should gladly exchange my place with any priest who should become my Superior. It is not desirable that everyone should know when I am in town." Then he adds: "Let [my replacement as superior] be a man such as your Lordship would designate for the highest office. I have already admirable subordinates."[4]

Garnet's last letter crossed Aquaviva's of July 16 from Mantua, which did not reach him until much later in the year. It contained the assurance of support that Garnet sought. Even before receiving news from Garnet, the General had learned of the loss of Southwell "with sincere and deep grief and with sorrow of heart and mind" at the sudden termination of his companion's apostolate.[5]

Aquaviva, on his return to Rome, dealt with the problems he had left unsettled at Mantua. "I have given much thought," he told Garnet in January 1593,

> to the question of substituting in your place another priest who will have charge of affairs in England and direct our work there. It is a serious issue. Your Reverence has now had much practice and experience and also has other qualities that are needed. You would seem still by far the best equipped person for the position.

Aware of the disappointment he was causing Garnet, he added:

> You must retain this burden yourself and with keenness. We have good reason to think that our decision will

---

[4] Ibid.

[5] Clement VIII, elected on January 29, 1592, had sent Aquaviva that year to settle a dispute between the dukes of Mantua and Parma. During his three months' absence from Rome, Aquaviva's enemies had persuaded the Pope to call an extraordinary general congregation with the purpose of obtaining his deposition. These months were the most critical in the General's long period of office.

turn out well. We are ready to send you, if they are
needed, more men to help you, discreet persons on
whom you can rely. We will take no further steps until
the time is safe for sailing and for transacting business.
Meanwhile we pray to the Lord that this year may be a
happy and propitious one for your Reverence and that
God through his abundant grace and consolation may
turn all to gladness and joy.[6]

Aquaviva, however, did make inquiries about the
suitability of an English Jesuit, Henry Walpole, then
working in Spain, to relieve Garnet of his office.

But Southwell was never long out of Garnet's
mind. "It truly seems," he was to write later,

that with a special providence our Lord willed to keep
him all that time [in the Tower] as it were in a good
noviceship, to prove him like gold in a furnace, to make
him worthy of Himself. Certainly so long a
perseverance, such a multitude of sufferings, such a lack
of all human aids and means, shows clearly how fortified
was that holy soul and furnished with spiritual weapons,
and at the same time with what power and love our
Lord spoke to his heart in that blessed solitude, giving
him vigour and freshness, and making him manifest in
public such peace and tranquillity.

This was Garnet's reflection after his companion
had been confined for thirty months in a solitary Tower
cell. During this time Southwell recovered his strength
slowly. But Topcliffe's treatment had left him with an
enduring injury. While he was hanging from the wall,
he had spewed a great quantity of blood, which led to a
serious intestinal trouble. When, after two and a half
years in the Tower, he was removed to Newgate to
await trial, "he asked the gaoler not to go too far away
in case some accident should happen to him or he

---

[6] C.A. to H.G. (June 9, 1593), Archives S.J., Rome: Fland.-
Belg. 1, f. 509.

should be in need of something, because as a result of his bitter tortures his sides were not strong enough for him to shout."[7]

Writing in another place of Southwell's period in the Tower, Garnet observed that all the time he

> was never once able to celebrate Mass or to confess himself or to speak with anyone who might bring him a little consolation, yet he came forth to judgment and execution with such an undaunted spirit, so calm and serene, that it seemed that he had been with a company of angelic souls and was about to enjoy himself at the rarest banquet.[8]

Often in his reflections he had turned to the theme of an early poem, "A Childe My Choyce," which summarizes his frequent meditations:

> I praise him most, I love him best, all praise and love is his
> While him I love, in him I live, and cannot live amiss.
>
> Love's sweetest mark, lauds' highest theme, man's most desired light:
> To love him, life: to leave him, death: to live in him, delight.
>
> He mine, by gift: I his, by debt : thus each to other due:
> First friend he was: best friend he is: all times will try him true.
>
> His knowledge rules: his strength defends: his love doth cherish all:
> His birth our joy: his life our light: his death our end of thrall.
>
> Almighty babe whose tender arms can force all foes to fly:
> Correct my faults, protect my life, direct me when I die.[9]

---

[7] H.G. to C.A. (May 15, 1593), F.G. 651.

[8] H.G. to C.A. (February 22, 1595), Archives S.J., Rome: Anglia, 31, I, ff. 107-8.

[9] *Poems*, 13.

With no further torture and with the comfort he derived from his reading of St. Bernard, Southwell's imprisonment in the Tower was a period of tranquillity. The food was bad, the air bad also, but this was little for him to endure. Solitary confinement, however, told on him. Under questioning at his trial, he answered, "I am decayed in memory with long and close confinement." It became known outside that by his gentle behavior he had won the affection of the lieutenant, who spoke of him as "that saint," saying that it was an honor to have had converse with him.[10]

There was an occasion when the lieutenant entering Southwell's cell was followed by the dog belonging to Philip Howard, earl of Arundel, confined in another part of the Tower. It was to him that Southwell in his early days in London had addressed the letters that he later gathered into his book *An Epistle of Comfort.* Southwell gave his blessing to the dog to take back to its master, but was never permitted to see Philip.

In March 1593, after eight months in the Tower, a rumor reached Garnet that Southwell had been tortured again and was about to be brought to trial, but it proved to be unfounded. Later the same month it was learned that several members of the Council, including Robert Cecil, had interrogated him at intervals about Thomas Bell, who had given up his priesthood at the end of 1592. Asked about him, Southwell said that he thought they would find him a man of average ability and given to quarreling. "So indeed we did," said one of the examiners to Garnet's informant, "for he turned out to be a most trivial and pestilent fellow, in contrast with this Southwell, who is so plainly earnest and devout."

---

[10] H.G. to C.A. (February 22, 1595), Archives S.J., Rome: Anglia, 31, I, ff. 107-8.

But there were numerous other occasions on which Southwell was examined. "He answered always," says Garnet, "with great shrewdness as well as with prudence."[11]

But no treasonable charge on which Southwell could be tried emerged from the early examinations, which concerned alleged or crazy plots against the Queen; and it was now even suggested that he might be banished with William Weston. Meanwhile, before the end of 1593 Garnet suffered another severe loss. Fr. Henry Walpole, after working for nine years among the English Catholics in Spain, was designated by Aquaviva to be superior of the mission, in accordance with the undertaking he had earlier given Garnet. But landing on the Yorkshire coast on December 4 that year, he was arrested the same evening. Technically he had not violated the law that a subject of the Queen ordained abroad and returning to England had to give himself up within twenty-four hours, but his plea was ignored. From York he was sent to the Tower, where he was racked fourteen times and subjected to other tortures in use there. He lay there in pain for months, his presence probably unknown to Southwell.

In the same winter, after numerous examinations Southwell sent a personal message to Sir Robert Cecil, asking either that he should be brought to trial to answer in public the slanders Topcliffe was propagating against him or that he should be allowed to see his friends. Eventually the first part of his petition was granted but not with the result he had intended.

On the occasion of one of the examinations, Southwell had expounded to Cecil the theory and legitimate practice of equivocation, which was used by

---

[11] H.G. to C.A., (March 17, 1593), Archives S.J., Rome: Anglia, I. II, f. 27.

both Puritans and Catholics to protect themselves against a system of enforced self-incrimination worse than anything devised by the Inquisition in Spain. Southwell was reported by Anne Bellamy to have told her that "if upon her oath she was asked whether she had seen a priest or not, she might lawfully say no, though she had seen one, keeping this meaning in her mind that she did not see any with intent to betray him."[12]

This explanation of equivocation, on which Southwell enlarged at his examination and again at his trial, gave the government the opportunity it was looking for to bring odium on Southwell and, worse, on the morals of the Catholic community. Without realizing it, Southwell had played into the hands of the Council, who through a skillful prosecutor could now demonstrate that the moral practices of Catholics were a danger to the stability of society. This was the charge that formed the brunt of the assault on him by the attorney general at his trial.

On February 18, 1595, Southwell was transferred from the Tower to his third prison, Newgate, to await trial. Garnet, who was back in London that month, received word of the change. Possibly forewarned, he watched his companion taken through the London streets that morning. Certainly he saw him two days later taken again by road from Newgate to Westminster Hall. He noted that, although Southwell during his months of captivity had not celebrated Mass or received any of the comforts of religion, he was so tranquil and recollected as he went to Westminster that he might have been stepping out of a religious house.

Garnet was taken by surprise by the suddenness of Southwell's arraignment. Knowing nothing of the

_____

[12] Ibid.

examinations by Cecil, he was convinced that Topcliffe had engineered the crisis. Garnet wrote that in Topcliffe's "insatiable fury" against Southwell, he "never ceased petitioning the Council to send him for trial. He was hoping always to appropriate the spoils of the Bellamy House at Uxenden where the Father had been taken and so endow his virtuous bride" (Anne Bellamy).[13]

Garnet gathered the details of his companion's three days and three nights in Newgate, reckoned the harshest of the twelve London prisons.

> He stayed there for three or four days, in Limbo, as they call it, a subterranean cell of evil repute where condemned felons await the hangman's stroke, yet a place honoured by many martyrs and by the conversion of several criminals through their conversation there with some valiant soldiers of Christ.[14]

This was Topcliffe's method of weakening his prisoner before trial without actually maiming him. But this time he was partially foiled by the kindness of Southwell's jailer. Garnet continues his account:

> But through the loving foresight of a Catholic and by the kindness of the keeper, [Robert] found it fitted with a bed and a fire and a constant supply of candles, for there is no other means of light in the place. All the time he was there, no felon was condemned so he was alone with the worms—except that the keeper came to visit him several times, a most unusual thing.

> On the first evening he arrived and all the time that followed, he was given such good fare that he said he had never eaten like this all the time he was in the Tower. . . . He was greeted with a cup of wine which he accepted, saying that it was the first time he had drunk wine for two years or more. It was the Catholics who

---

[13] Stonyhurst: Anglia II, 41.

[14] H.G. to C.A. (February 22, 1595), F.G. 651.

procured these things for him as a sign of the great love they bore him, and they would gladly have done much more if it had been allowed them.

Just before he was brought out for trial he was visited by a little old woman sent by his friends with a cup of soup, who said to him, "O Sir, God comfort you, you must appear today before the judges. But drink up this, it will make you merry and brave." He drank it and said to her, "This is broth for champions, not for condemned men." And that was the first news he had that his hour had come.

He was then conducted to that same tribunal called the King's Bench, where so many years before had stood his blessed predecessor, Edmund Campion.[15]

---

[15] Ibid.

NINE

How Will You Be Tried?

No announcement of the trial had been made. Not even the keeper knew the day. But it became clear afterwards that Southwell was kept in Newgate as long as it took to create a diversion in London. On the day he was brought to Westminster Hall, a notorious criminal was led to Tyburn with all the public notice that could be arranged. "Almost all the city," Garnet writes, "went out to see the execution and knew nothing of what was happening to Father Robert."[1] Yet, in spite of this, a number of Catholics got word and watched him brought to trial with halberds and bills, and with his arms tied with a thong. As he came to the bar, they loosed his hands, and he doffed his hat and made obeisance to the Bench.

In spite of his more lenient treatment in the Tower, Southwell was a broken man of thirty-three. His memory was failing, he was afraid of his own physical weakness, but remained serene, loving, and courteous to all with the single exception of his tormentor Topcliffe. "God forgive me, Mr. Topcliffe," he was soon to thrust at him for the last time, "but I do not think there can be another man like you in the whole king-

---

[1] H.G. to C.A. (February 22, 1595), F.G. 651.

dom."[2] Gerard, who himself suffered at Topcliffe's hands a few years later, could not bring himself to be civil to him when he remembered what Southwell had suffered at his hands. "By God's ordinance," Gerard wrote, Southwell "was delivered over to encounter hand to hand the cruellest tyrant in all England, Topcliffe, a man most infamous and hateful to all the realm for his bloody and butcherly mind."[3] He was present now at Westminster Hall, determined to see Southwell condemned and to assist the prosecution should it need help.

Facing Southwell was the chief justice of the Queen's Bench, Sir John Popham, a huge, coarse, sprawling, ugly man, whom Garnet had known between leaving Winchester and going to Rome, when he had been an apprentice to Richard Tottel, the printer of law books. Garnet had described him as someone "detested by all classes . . . and prepared to inflict extremities of injustice on poor Catholics."[4] Over against him was the handsome attorney general, Sir Edward Coke, the cleverest and richest lawyer in England, ready to turn to his advantage all that Southwell had explained to Cecil on equivocation.

The case opened with the now customary recital by the chief justice of all the plots, real and fictitious, against the Queen, starting with the "rebellion in the north . . . stirred by Cardinal Allen, a Jesuit," down to the time Southwell was in the Tower, omitting only the Babington Plot; for Popham had read *An Humble Supplication,* in which Southwell had exposed the

---

[2] Ibid.

[3] John Gerard, "A Narrative of the Gunpowder Plot," ed. John Morris, in *Condition of English Catholics* (London, 1871), 18.

[4] Ibid.

conspiracy as fictitious. These facts the jury was asked to bear in mind when considering their verdict.

The bill of indictment was then read. It asserted that the prisoner was a priest ordained abroad and had been present "like a false traitor" at Uxenden on July 26, 1592.[5]

"How will you be tried?" asked Popham; "by God and by your country?"

"By God and by you, for I would not lay upon my country the guilt of my condemnation," answered Southwell, aware that his case had been prejudged.

"We are not to try you. You are to be tried 'by God and the laws.'"

"By God I will be tried, but not by the law, for the law is contrary to the law of God."

Popham cut Southwell short. "If you refuse the trial, it shall be a sufficient condemnation, and in that case we are to proceed with you otherwise."

Pointing to the jurors, Southwell retorted, "I am loth that these poor men should be guilty of my death. But if you will needs have treason that I must lay upon, I will be tried by God and the country."

Asked whether he wished to challenge any of the jurors before they were sworn in, he answered, "I know no goodness in any of them, neither do I know any harm, but according to charity I will judge the best and will challenge none."

---

[5] The account of R.S.'s trial is taken from the following often overlapping sources: (1) *A briefe Discource of the condemnation of Mr Robert Southwell,* by an unknown eyewitness: see Stonyhurst: Anglia, 31, 1; (2) H.G.'s two Italian letters, February 22 and March 7, 1595, Archives S.J., Rome: Anglia 31, 1; (3) "The Relation of Thomas Leake, a Secular Priest": Stonyhurst: Anglia VI, printed in C.R.S., 5:333–36; (4) H.G. to C.A. (May 1, 1595), F.G. 651.

It caused Southwell pain to raise his voice, but it made no difference; for there was little chance that he would be permitted to make a straight speech without interruption, especially in a trial of this kind with Top-cliffe present to assist the prosecution.

The attorney general was anxious to make the trial an occasion for advancing his career. He began quietly rehearsing the items in the indictment. When he came to the point that the prisoner had been made a priest since the first year of the Queen's reign, he added that he had not been born when Her Majesty came to the throne.

Here Popham interjected, seeming to despise the prisoner for his youth, "How old are you?"

Southwell replied softly, "I think I am near the age of our Saviour who lived upon the earth thirty-three years."

At this Topcliffe made a great exclamation, then blurted out that Southwell was comparing himself to Christ.

"No, no!" the discomfited Southwell tried to call out. "Christ is my creator and I am a worm created by him."

Then Coke continuing his speech came to the act that forbade such priests as Southwell entering the kingdom. "I know the act," said Southwell, "but it is impossible to make any such law agreeable to the word of God."

This made Coke raise his voice threateningly. Once more Southwell had to listen to the recital of the litany of plots with which Popham had begun proceed-ings, but this time in more vivid detail. Then the attor-ney enlarged on the corruption of the commonwealth threatened by the publication of illicit books. Whenever he paused momentarily, Southwell tried to interrupt him.

"Hold your peace," interjected Topcliffe, "until the Queen's Council has spoken."

This gave Southwell the chance he had been waiting for. "My Lord," he said, "let me answer forthwith. I am decayed in memory with long and close imprisonment and I have been tortured ten times. I had rather endured ten executions."

This threw the court into confusion.

"I never heard that you were tortured," said Popham.

"I never knew that you were racked," said Coke.

"If he were racked, let me die for it," said Topcliffe in support of the attorney.

"No," Southwell answered, "but you have another kind of torture, I think, worse than the rack." He then described how he had been treated in his tormentor's private prison; but when Popham maintained that other nations acted in the same way, Southwell admitted this, adding, "But when by torture nothing can be got, I wish there might be some measure therein lest by extremity of pain a man be driven, if it were possible, to despair." Then, turning to those watching the trial, he pleaded, "I speak not this for myself but for others lest they be handled so inhumanly as I."

In an attempt to prove himself innocent, Topcliffe called to Southwell, "Show the marks of your tortures."

Southwell turned on him, "Ask a woman to show her throes."

Topcliffe had no answer. He blurted out, "I did but set him against a wall. I had authority to use him as I did, so that I did not hurt life or limb. I have the Council's letters to show for it"; and he spoke at length to clear himself of the accusations laid against him.

"Thou art a bad man," were the last words South-well addressed to him.

Here Coke came in, "Mr. Topcliffe has no need to go about to excuse his proceedings in the manner of his torturings"; and turning to Southwell he said mean-ingfully, "Think you that you will not be tortured? Yea, we will tear the hearts out of a hundred of your bodies."

"I will blow you to pieces," shouted Topcliffe.

"What all?" asked Southwell; "soul and body too?"

Coke now called his first witness. It was Anne Bellamy. After being sworn in, she made her statement about what she claimed, correctly or not, Southwell had told her about denying if necessary that she had seen a priest when she had in fact actually seen one.

"This is a doctrine," Coke called to the jurors, "by which all judgement, all giving of testimonies shall be perverted."

Southwell was taken off his guard. Perhaps to save the Bellamy family from shame, he did not ques-tion Anne's credentials as a witness; she was the moth-er of Topcliffe's child. Instead he said that his words were not exactly as she had given them but were true in substance.

"Perjury!" shouted Coke. "Listen to the doctrine of the Jesuits. It is lawful to commit perjury!"

Topcliffe came in with his support: "And to Rob-ert Cecil he confessed it and sought to excuse it from Scripture."

Southwell pleaded that if he were given the chance to explain his meaning,

> he would show that it was agreeable to the word of God, to the laws both canon and civil, and was not his own opinion only, but the opinion of the Doctors and Fathers of the Church, and according to the policies and

proceedings of all ages and in all Christian nations; and that if they should not admit that, they should take away the government of all states, both ecclesiastical and temporal, yea, and the secrecy of man, and that, without it, neither this state nor any other state, government or policy could possibly stand.

But he was given no chance to explain. Whenever he began he was interrupted by Coke. Now he abandoned the attempt and prayed. The impudent reply came in answer to his prayer.

"Mr. Attorney," he challenged Coke, "you must admit my doctrine or else I will prove you no good subject or friend of the Queen."

"Yea?" inquired Coke; "let me hear that."

Southwell held the trump card again. He began his defense thus:

Suppose that the French King should invade her Majesty's realm and that she (which God forbid) were enforced to fly to some private house for safety from her enemies, where none knew her being but Mr. Attorney. Suppose that Mr. Attorney, being taken, were put upon his oath to say whether she were there or not. And suppose (for such would be the case) that Mr. Attorney's refusal to swear should be held as a confession of her being in the house, would Mr. Attorney refuse to swear? Or would he say, "She is not there," meaning "I intend not to tell you"?

The parallel was exact to the last detail. There was silence in the court. Southwell had proved his teaching by example more convincingly than he might have done by resort to Doctors and to Scripture. One report on Southwell's trial says the attorney "remained as one struck by apoplexy."

Southwell became bolder: "If Mr. Attorney should refuse to swear, I say he were neither Her Majesty's good subject nor her friend."

Popham intervened to help Coke, who had no answer. "He should refuse to swear," he said.

"Then," replied Southwell, "that were by silence to betray her Majesty."

Coke recovered quickly. He refused to allow the parallel between the two cases and losing his temper called Southwell a "boy-priest," telling him that he had not read the Doctors. But Southwell was again quick with his answer. "I have read those who have read them and you, Mr. Attorney, in the study of your laws do not go always to the ground and principles of the law, but take other men's reports."

"Aye," said Coke, "you have studied the Doctors. You have studied Doctor Allen, Doctor Persons, Doctor Holt, Doctor Traitor—" Topcliffe joined in the abuse and, as Persons wrote, many times they called him "boy-priest" *(sacerdote putto)* with much railing.

After reading later this exchange, John Deckers, his boyhood friend, noted that this answer of Southwell to Coke was proof of his effortless superiority: "He was in truth very learned in the Doctors, having studied them closely for twelve years. He preferred, however, not to waste the fine steel of his mind in a war of insults, but instead, like David with Goliath, wrested away his enemy's sword and cut his throat with it."

Popham intervened again, this time with a more reasoned objection to Southwell's doctrine. "Mr. Southwell," he said, "if this doctrine were allowed, it would supplant all justice, for we are men and not gods, and can judge but according to men's outward actions and speeches, and not according to their secret and inward intentions.

Southwell attempted to answer this fair objection. "Two things," he replied, "are to be presupposed in this cause; first, that the refusing to swear is held as a confessing the thing, and second, that the oath is minis-tered by such as have no lawful authority, for every oath ought to contain judgement, justice and truth, and no man is bound to answer every man that asketh him unless it were a competent judge—" But again South-well's explanation was ruined by repeated interruptions. Once more Topcliffe started to rail. Finally Popham called him to order, then after a brief address to the jury, sent them out to consider their verdict.

In a poem entitled "Prodigall Chyld's Soule Wracke," Southwell had expressed earlier what he must have felt during his trial:

> I found myself on every side
>   Enwrapped in waves of woe,
> And tossed with a toilsome tide,
>   Could to no port for refuge go.
>
> The wrestling winds with raging blasts
>   Still hold me in a cruel chase
> They break my anchors, sails and masts,
>   Permitting no reposing place.
>
> The boisterous seas with swelling floods
>   On every side did work their spite.
> Heaven, overcast with stormy clouds,
>   Denied the planets' guiding light.[6]

After the jury had left, Southwell leaned for sup-port on the dock. Popham asked him whether he wished to retire and refresh himself with a cordial. But Southwell begged to stay. There were friends of his in the hall who had been following the proceedings, and no doubt he wished to acknowledge their presence and be with them, albeit at a distance, after his months of solitary confinement.

---

[6] *Poems,* 43.

When the jury returned after fifteen minutes, the clerk asked Southwell whether he had any reason why judgment should not be pronounced. The people, Garnet was told, were hoping that he would make a speech. But all he said was, "I pray God forgive all that are in any way accessories to my death."

But even now Topcliffe would not let Southwell alone. "I found him hiding in the tiles," he said mockingly, referring to his capture. Southwell was not lost for an answer. It was he who raised the last laugh. "It was time to hide," he said, "when Mr. Topcliffe came."

The account of the trial continues:

> Topcliffe not being suffered to reply the Lord Chief Justice . . . gave judgement that Southwell should be carried to Newgate from whence he came, and from thence to be drawn to Tyburn upon a hurdle, and there to be hanged and cut down alive, his bowels to be burned before his face, his head to be stricken off, his body to be quartered and disposed of at her Majesty's pleasure.
>
> Mr. Southwell thereunto made low and humble reverence and gave great thanks for it. The Chief Justice wished that some Minister might have conference with him and said he would send a learned preacher unto him. Mr. Southwell answered, "As for that, you need not take any care."

Southwell's hands were again fastened. Before he was led out by his guard, there was a debate whether he should be taken back to Newgate by road or sent to the Tower by water, in order to avoid a demonstration of sympathy by a crowd who, in spite of the diversion to draw them away, had gathered outside the hall. In the end they concluded that he would "go quiet enough and so he went joyfully . . . through the streets." Garnet, who was probably there, describes the scene. "His Catholic friends came to meet him at different places on the way; they crossed the road to see him and counted themselves happy if they were able to catch a glance from him. The Father, inasmuch as he was able, indicated that he recognised them." Another account adds that the crowd remarked that he seemed "full of consolation, his countenance nothing dismayed, they never knowing him to look better or more cheerfully."

TEN

INTO YOUR HANDS

B ack in Newgate Southwell was returned to the underground dungeon where he had awaited his trial. That afternoon some ministers argued with him on points of religion, but there is no report of what passed between them. It can be assumed that Southwell was courteous and that an account of their conversations was given to the Council; for still the Queen would have greatly preferred his conversion to his execution. Other preachers came that night. All that Catholics could learn was that Southwell's keeper swore that he had never heard "so rare a man" and that he himself henceforth would lead a better life for the saving of his soul. Thanks to him, Southwell's friends were able to send him some dainty dish, which he ate heartily, sending back a message to say that they had given him food fit for royalty. The only strident note was struck by the head keeper who warned him against any attempt at suicide. "Did you ever hear of a Catholic priest who hurt himself so?" asked Southwell. "Why should we add the destruction of our soul to the death of our body?"[1]

---

[1] The sources for this chapter are the same as in chapter 9, n. 5.

There were others who came and went. "What was further done and said that night was kept very secret and known to very few."

But Garnet gathered every detail he could of that last night. He learned that after the last caller had left, sleep eluded Southwell; his mind was at peace, but scorpions and other creatures pestered him until morning. Remaining awake, he prayed. His course was all but finished. He had sought courageously to defend himself. His uncertainties were over. He had not coveted condemnation but had welcomed it when inevitably it came.

When his friendly keeper came to tell him that it was now daybreak, he threw his arms round him, embraced him, and thanked him for his courtesy. "No man ever brought me such good news before," he told him. "And, alas, I have nothing to give you except this." He then took off his cap. "If I had anything better to give you, you should have it," he assured him. There were Catholics who offered to purchase the cap from the keeper but "albeit a Protestant he maketh such account of it that he can be brought by no means to forego it."

The horses were already harnessed. Before he was strapped on to the hurdle, he was offered a posset. "It was good," he said as he returned the cup. "It has made my heart glad."

As he was bound to the hurdle that had taken so many of his fellow priests to Tyburn, he exclaimed, "How great a preferment is this for so base a servant." An old countryman who was passing by cried out to him, "God in heaven bless and strengthen you." When told to be silent, the man continued his prayer aloud for Southwell. On the road a gentlewoman, a cousin, whom he had once visited in prison, saluted him, asking for his prayers. "Good cousin," he was able to say,

"I thank you. I pray you pray for me." As she continued alongside, Southwell cautioned her to keep clear of him and of the horses that were drawing the hurdle, fearful that her devotion might lead to her arrest again. He told her to leave him and then blessed her as well as he could with his bound hands. For the rest of the painful journey, he remained in silent prayer with his eyes lifted to heaven. Passing St. Giles-in-the-Fields, he continued along the road west until he reached the gallows at Tyburn.

As he was untied from the hurdle, he was helped to his feet. "His courage and nobility and gentleness," wrote Garnet, "the beauty of his face and form so won the hearts of all that even the mob of sight-seers gave it as their verdict that this was the properest man they have ever seen that came to Tyburn for hanging."

He was helped to the floor of the cart. With a handkerchief between his bound arms he wiped the mud from his face and neck; then, looking out to the crowd, he rolled it up into a ball and threw it to an acquaintance whom he recognized below the gallows. As the hangman opened his doublet, Southwell asked and was given leave to address the people. Making the sign of the cross, he began, "Whether we live or whether we die, we belong to Christ"; it was the text he must have used in many sermons to his friends. Abruptly the undersheriff who was supervising the execution interrupted him, saying that he should cry for God's mercy and make an end. "Give me leave to speak," Southwell pleaded. The crowd clearly wanted to hear him, so he was able to continue.

> I am brought here to perform the last act of this miserable life, and for that my time is very short. I do most humbly desire at the hands of Almighty God for our Saviour Jesus' sake that he would vouchsafe to pardon and forgive all my sins. . . . As concerning the Queen's Majesty, God Almighty knoweth that I never meant or

intended harm or evil against her, and yet in this short
time that I have to live I most humbly beseech and
desire Almighty God for his tender mercy's sake . . .
that he would vouchsafe she may so use those gifts and
graces which God, nature and fortune hath bestowed on
her that with them she may both please and glorify
God, advance the happiness of our country and purchase to herself the preservation and salvation of her
body and soul.

Next I commend into the hands of Almighty God my
poor country, desiring Him for his infinite mercy's sake
to reduce it to such perfect insight, knowledge and understanding of his truth that thereby its people may
learn to praise and glorify God and gain their souls'
health and eternal salvation.

Then, after asking the people to pray for his perseverance to the end, he concluded: "I do acknowledge
and confess that I am a priest of the Catholic and Roman Church (I thank God most highly for it) and of
the Society of Jesus."

When Southwell was finished, the hangman
stripped him of his shirt, put the halter round his neck
and fastened it to the gallows. It was then that the
minister attending the execution spoke.

You hold the decrees of the Council of Trent, wherein
is decreed that no man shall presume to believe that he
is sure to be saved, but is to doubt. Now, if you believe
to be saved, you contradict the Council; but if you
doubt, being to die, your case is hard, and your doubt-
ing, we must needs doubt.

It was no time or day for theological subtleties.
"Good Mr. Minister," pleaded Southwell, courteous to
the end, "give me leave and trouble me not. Notwith-
standing your words I hope to be saved by the death
and passion of our Saviour." The Minister was for
going on, but the crowd growled and protested: "Let

him alone! He has prayed for the Queen. Let that suffice!"

It was the hangman who saved him from further debate. He lifted Southwell's chin for the noose to settle. Southwell was heard to pray softly: "Blessed Mary, ever a Virgin, and all you angels and saints assist me. *In manus tuas, Domine, commendo animam meam*" (Into your hands, O Lord, I commend my spirit). These were to have been his last words, but the hangman delayed. At first there was only a small jerk as the cart was taken away. The rope was readjusted and the knot, which was tied too large, was slipped right behind his head, forcing it forward and downward. Southwell repeated the prayer In manus tuas.

Then suddenly he opened his eyes and, as if his soul were already in heaven, he looked at the people "with a most lovely countenance" or, as another account has it, "like the sun when it breaketh forth after it hath dispersed the clouds." His voice was heard clearly as he recited the psalm Miserere. Then again he was heard saying, "In manus tuas . . ." for the third time.

Three times also the sheriff's men came forward to cut the rope, and each time the people cried out, "Stay! Stay!" Lord Mountjoy, later the viceroy of Ireland, standing below the gallows, held them back. "Let him hang until he is dead," they called out. "Pull his legs!" This was to shorten his agony.

The hangman obeyed, then took Southwell's body into his hands "with great courtesy." As it was being disembowelled, the heart leaped in the hangman's hands and again after it was cast into the cauldron. When the head was cut off and held up to the crowd, no one cried "Traitor," but many signed themselves with the cross.

As the hangman continued with his task, some Catholics, seeming to pass by casually, offered him money for a piece of bone or a lock of hair, or managed to dip a handkerchief in the martyr's blood.

After Southwell's death a story was told about events during his last night before execution that were "kept very secret and known to very few." His earliest biographer tells it thus:

> After the Father had been sentenced to death there came to him in his prison an English nobleman of high rank, who besought him earnestly, as he was now to quit this life, to tell him whether that was true which he had been charged with, namely that he had come to detach subjects from their obedience to the Queen. To this the Father replied that his intention had never been anything but the eternal good of souls; that so far from repenting what he had done, he would do it again if he could; that he would come again, and many times more, not only from Rome but from the farthest parts of the world, to procure the salvation of the Queen, which he desired no less than his own; that he had always asked the Lord God to enlighten her, and her Council also, as to the error they were in, and not to hold them guilty for his death.

> The noble, very much moved by his answer, departed; and he went and told the Queen all that had [later] passed at the death of the Father praising him very much, and the rare parts he was gifted with. When the Queen had heard him, she replied that they had deceived her with calumnies telling her that the Father had come to the realm to raise sedition; and she showed signs of grief for his death, especially when she saw a book that he had composed in the English tongue on different topics, pious and devout, designed to teach poets how to safeguard their talent and employ it as befitted.[2]

[2] Diego Yepez, *Historia Particular de la Persecucion de Inglaterra* (Madrid, 1599). See Devlin, 317f. The book mentioned

The nobleman was Lord Mountjoy, the Queen's favorite, a man deeply interested in literature. It was he who held back the hangman when the crowd had shouted "Stay." And also, when the sheriff, holding up Southwell's head, got no reply to his cry "Traitor" and had shouted, "I see there are some here who have come, not to honour the Queen but to reverence a traitor," it was Mountjoy who spoke for all: "I cannot answer for his religion, but I wish to God that my soul may be with his."

---

here would have been either *Saint Peter's Complaint* or, less likely, *Mary Magdalen's Tears.*

ELEVEN

VALOR, CONSTANCY, AND DEVOTION

Garnet was relieved that his companion's sufferings were at an end. On February 22, the day after the execution, he wrote to Aquaviva:

> Whether I should be sorry now or glad, I do not know. My sorrow is that I have lost my most dear and loved companion; my gladness, that the man I have cherished so much has risen to the throne of God, where he will be given the recompense earned by his labours—peace in return for his cares, and the immense happiness of his God in exchange for his unspeakable tortures. And so it is more surely fitting to rejoice, and for the Church, for your Lordship and for me to give solemn thanks to God.[1]

After finishing this letter to Aquaviva, Garnet found time for another the same day. His courier had not yet arrived. In this second letter he speaks more eloquently about "this unvanquished soldier of Christ, my most faithful subject and the bravest of martyrs, once my closest companion and brother, now my patron, lord and ruler together with Christ in his empire."[2] He closed with a request for Aquaviva's prayers

---

[1] H.G. to C.A. (February 22, 1595), F.G. 651.

[2] H.G. to C.A., second letter of the same date, Stonyhurst:

that his own sins might not hold him back from the contest or, in the midst of it, make him less brave than his companion.

Southwell's heroic death heartened Garnet. If ever there was a martyr, it was Southwell, and Garnet was proud of his close association with him. He was convinced also that it would only be a short time before his companion was recognized as one of the great heroes of the universal Church. With this conviction he wrote next month a yet longer letter. Although he addressed it to Aquaviva, he intended it to be passed on to his Roman friends. "I shall write in Italian," he explained, "so as to give pleasure to my dear brethren who do not understand Latin,"[3] for Southwell's life concerned all Jesuits, Brothers and priests, and especially those in Rome, "where he lived and was brought up among his brethren there, receiving from them so many loving services." Moreover, in this way Garnet could give proof of his own special affection for them all. "I think of them and speak of them with the greatest comfort to myself, and I have deep confidence in their holy prayers, for I am assured that they have not forgotten me." He apologized for his mistakes in Italian, for "after my absence of nine years I have forgotten a large part of the little I once knew."

Throughout the following spring and summer, Garnet's thoughts returned frequently to the good name of his martyr companion. He was impatient to get assurance that his long Italian letter with the account of his martyrdom had reached Rome. By May 1 he had received no acknowledgement and began to fear that it had been intercepted: there were, in fact, reports that certain papers of his "had fallen into the enemy's

---

Anglia, II, 4; also Stonyhurst: Grene P. 566.

[3] H.G. to C.A. (March 7, 1595), F.G. 651.

hands." It had been his intention to remain silent until he was certain that his letters were reaching Rome, but now he had fresh details to add. If the government wanted to intercept his correspondence, it could," he wrote defiantly. "We will be no less persistent in writing to you than they are in persecuting us." Aquaviva had no reason to fear he would commit any indiscretion.

> I will uncover nothing that is hidden. I shall not commit secrets to writing nor divulge what is done in darkness, but all the cruel, barbarous and bestial acts perpetrated under the noonday sun, these I shall make known on the summit of the Capitoline hill. Therein is our triumph, our crown and our laurels. Have they intercepted my letter about my dear Robert? If so, I shall write again. His valor, constancy and devotion are not such as can be lost to memory should a single letter fall into the enemy's hands, unless there is obliterated at one and the same time all that is written with such splendor in the hearts of all who knew him.[4]

What throws light on Garnet's own character is his appraisal of Southwell as his subject. Southwell's virtues as a religious priest were known to all who lived with him. From his own dealings with him, he could say that Southwell had never lost the first fervor of his religious life. His friends among the laity who knew him well had often seen him in tears because his superior had never in his life given him a command or even counseled him. This Southwell put down to Garnet's consideration of his weakness and had concluded that he had not sufficient reliance on his virtue to give him a direct order. It made him sad. But "the truth was this, that I never saw in him," wrote Garnet,

> anything fractious or obstinate. Therefore I allowed him always to act as he himself thought best. And his judge-

---

[4] H.G. to C.A. (May 1, 1595), F.G. 651. the next three quotations are from this same source.

ment was always right. Over the many years that we
lived together in such harmony of mind in the midst of
great difficulties there was never the least shadow of
difference between us. And I attribute this to his virtue.

Although no poet himself, Garnet appreciated his
companion's literary gifts and claimed that he not
merely equaled but surpassed many profane authors
and poets and had shown them how they might turn
their talent from lascivious to religious and serious
subjects. Then he comes close to revealing that he was
present at the execution. It was a novel sight in London
to see the way the executioners, instead of dragging
him to the quartering block, carried him there with
great reverence. Then he summed up everything he had
seen or heard, saying, "His manliness, his nobility,
meekness and handsome appearance won all hearts so
that in the judgement of the common crowd no man
like him had ever been hanged at Tyburn." Indeed, it
was not until five years later that the authorities dared
bring another priest to Tyburn for execution. "I have a
rosary," Garnet told Aquaviva, "which he threw from
the scaffold and also the bone of one of his knees, and
these I shall send to your Lordship [as relics] when I
conveniently can." Nothing, meanwhile, would give him
more pleasure, he hints gently to Aquaviva, than to
learn that his Italian letter had arrived safely.

At first Southwell, unburdened by office, had been
more spontaneous in his letters to the General—he had
written merely as a friend, recording both trivial and
important events without a moment's doubt that Aquaviva would be equally interested in both—strange por-
tents at sea, a mishap to the *Revenge,* the appearance
of three prophets—Coppinger, the "prophet of mercy,"
proclaiming terrible judgments for evil-doers, his companion Arlington, "the prophet of judgement," and the
third, Hackett, "king of the earth, King of Christen-

dom, descended from heaven to execute judgement on those who refuse his mercy."[5]

The excitement both priests felt in their work was heightened by their anticipation of Aquaviva's interest in every aspect of their adventures. "Your Lordship will excuse me if I write less frequently than I should," Garnet once wrote when communications with Rome were difficult. "You must be assured that it is a great pleasure for me to write. No privation can affect me more than the loss of the facilities I once had of writing as frequently as I wished."[6]

From the time of Southwell's capture to his own last day of freedom, Garnet's letters, some long, some short, became more frequent. The pleasure it gave him to pour out his feelings on paper to Aquaviva compensated a little for the loss of Southwell's company. It is clear that from now on he seldom read what he had written; sometimes he is ungrammatical, nearly always he is hurried, always anxious to hand his Roman letters to the courier before the ink is dry. Whenever he sees an opportunity of dispatching a letter, he takes it whether he has much or little to say. Never is there any doubt in his mind of the friendship of Aquaviva, shared with Southwell, and his deep affection for them both on the mission for which the General himself had once volunteered. No matter what slanders and ill reports of him were later to reach Rome, Garnet had no doubt that Aquaviva would never falter in his trust and esteem of him.

It was this knowledge that helped to support him when on May 3, 1606, eight years after the execution of Southwell at Tyburn, he himself mounted the scaffold in St. Paul's churchyard and suffered the same death for the same cause as had his close companion.

---

[5] R.S. to C.A. (January 16, 1590), C.R.S., 5:329.

[6] H.G. to C.A. (March 2, 1590), Stonyhurst: Grene P. 555.

INDEX